THE BEST OF

OF

VOLUME 2

A *Sphere* Book

First published in Great Britain 1990 by
Sphere Books Ltd

ISBN 0 7474 0669 5

Reproduced, printed and bound in Great Britain by
BPCC Hazell Books
Aylesbury, Bucks, England
Member of BPCC Ltd.

Sphere Books Ltd
A Division of
Macdonald & Co (Publishers) Ltd
Orbit House
1 New Fetter Lane
London EC4A 1AR
A member of Maxwell Macmillan Pergamon Publishing Corporation

THE BEST OF SUNDAY SPORT

VOLUME 2

LOCH NESS MONSTER IS NAZI U-BOAT

SPHERE BOOKS LIMITED

HITLER

BON

FO

O

BRTI

ERKILL

RUBBER
PLANTS
SPROUT
CONDOM

FO

SAU

BUILDER
GIVES BIRTH
TO NINJA
TURTLE

OLD GRAN
DUSTBIN F

ER JOBBIE TUR

YOBME INTO

ZOMBIE

HUNGRY SOU

ATE MY

BAGPIPES

TRIED TO

BLOW

ME AW

FUCK OFF! CRU

IN

AGE

PEST

SEX

NY LIVES IN

R 18 YEARS

OLD GRANNY LIVES IN DUSTBIN FOR 18 YEARS

...and she refuses to leave her rancid home for new flat

By Home Affairs reporter BERTIE OLLOCKS

Star wars as US aces fight aliens

U.S. fighter pilots have been flying on suicide missions to destroy invading alien warships, a secret White House dossier has revealed.

According to informed Pentagon sources, the airmen have been chasing fleets of flying saucers – under orders from the CIA.

None of the pilots or craft has ever returned after the Star Wars battles.

Barry Greenwood, boss of the Citizens Against UFO Secrecy movement, said last night: "If pilots are disappearing under such circumstances we want to know about it. There must not be a cover up."

Tycoon gives his missus the bird...

TYCOON Oscar Wenner is divorcing his bird-brained missus, Greta . . . after she SUCKED UP his prize budgie in a VACUUM CLEANER!

Accident-prone Greta was cleaning the living room when Diego flew off his perch and was chewed up by the Hoover.

"The suction stopped for a second and I saw something squirming up the hose," said the 42-year-old housewife.

Rage

When he got home Oscar, 46, flew into a rage and filed a lawsuit to end their 12-year marriage.

He had shelled out £6,500 to jet Diego from South America to their home in Essen, Germany.

"I overlooked a lot— but I can't overlook Diego's death," said Oscar.

Eeee, beef bayonets!

A BARMY army is going into battle today...using BLACK PUDDINGS!

The nutty knights will re-enact the English Civil War but use their BEEF bayonets instead.

The silly soldiers will hurl black puddings at their enemies who will be armed with Yorkshire puds at the Corner Pin pub, Ramsbottom, Lancashire.

GROTTY Gran Greta Webber sucked an old kipper skin last night and sat proudly in her home...a battered RUBBISH SKIP!

SKIPPER...Greta

The tragic gap-toothed old crone has lived in the FOUL-SMELLING bin for an incredible 18 YEARS!

She dosses down on a rotting mass of old fish-heads, rusty cans and newspapers — and shelters from the rain under plastic bags. But the barmy BATTLEAXE was fighting mad after her local council slapped an EVICTION notice on her. She shrieked: "I LIKE it here."

Angry OAP Greta, 88, stormed: "This is my home and I'm staying.

"I don't pay rent. And I get free meals when the GARBAGE men come.

"I had a whole chicken carcase the other day and there was enough meat on it to feed a FAMILY."

Shocked health officials have pleaded with the authorities to find the potty pensioner a flat.

But the batty battler got punchy when the do-gooders called. She SPAT: "They can b****r off! I'll only leave in a WOODEN OVER-COAT.

Bedding

"I'm not taking up space anyone wants. I like being independent and I find loads of interesting things dumped here — clothes, food, books, you name it."

The wacky British-born wrinkly thinks rubbish is ART...and she decorates her home in Tampa, Florida.

The potty OAP boasted: "People think I'm CRAZY. But, in years to come, I'll be famous like Van Gogh."

IT'S OFFICIAL: Soviet boffins confirm space

WE KNEW IT

...but Russia's 12ft aliens visited America FIRST!

MOSCOW, Monday – Soviet scientists have confirmed the landing of an alien spaceship manned by giant people with tiny heads, the official Soviet news agency Tass said today.

NEWS FLASH . . . how the Press Association news agency broke the amazing story to the country

STUNNED UFO experts last night CONFIRMED the alien spaceship which invaded Russia has also been seen in America . . . as the world reeled at the official Soviet report that the craft landed in a major Commie city.

The huge glowing ball touched down in a park in agricultural Voronezh, leaving behind two strange stones which experts now believe are . . . ALIEN EGGS.

And today Sunday Sport publishes what the world has been waiting for — the first PHOTOGRAPH of the spaceship.

The UFO landed before a crowd of terrified Commies who watched as a hatch opened and three 12ft-tall, THREE-EYED spacemen stepped out wearing SILVER UNDERWEAR.

TASS news agency — the official mouthpiece of Gorbechev's ruling Communist Party — said the aliens made a boy DISAPPEAR into thin air with the blast from a giant laser gun.

The shocked ten-year-old suddenly materialised again after the craft blasted back into space leaving two cosmic rocks where it had landed.

Now, after a painstaking probe in both Russia and America, Sunday Sport investigators have traced reports of the SAME craft plaguing an American town for three months in 1986.

Pilot was grabbed by aliens

A YOUNG pilot, who vanished in mid-air being chased by a cigar-shaped object, was seized by ALIENS, experts revealed last night.

Their sensational findings show that 20-year-old Frederick Valentich was abducted on a flight from Melbourne to a nearby island.

Now 11 years later NASA physicist and author Richard Haines says he has proof that aliens were responsible.

The experts heard a recording of Valentich's chilling last message to Air Traffic Control.

''It is a long shape with a green light. And it is metallic-like, all shiny,'' he said.

In his book The Melbourne Episode — Case Study of a Missing Pilot, Haines says the pilot started panicking and shouted: ''That strange aircraft is hovering over me again.''

GORBYSMACKED...Soviet leader

By RAY LEVINE somewhere in RUSSIA

And when shown our WORLD EXCLUSIVE picture of the ship hovering above Belleville, Wisconsin, both the Yanks and the Reds agreed the spaceships are IDENTICAL.

"There is no doubt that is the same ship as the one I chased in my police car," said cop Geoff Kazmar from Belleville.

"Even from a distance, you could tell its size was awsome."

With blue lights flashing, the shocked cop and his partner gave chase.

But the ship outran them and disappeared over the horizon in seconds.

US Air Force investigators conceded that an unidentified ship had appeared on their screens at the time Geoff said he saw the craft.

Experts back our discovery

Meanwhile, a crack squad of Spetsnaz — the Russian equivalent of the SAS — sealed off the landing site in Voronezh as Soviet space experts moved in.

After checking to see whether the stones — which have now been confirmed as ET EGGS — were radioactive they were loaded into insulated steel boxes and taken to the Glavcosmos Institute in Moscow.

Alien life forms — similiar to HUMAN intestines — inside the rocks were revealed in the secret Soviet space agency's X-ray room.

The eggs were immediately transported in an INCUBATOR to another Glavcosmos base in the deep Urals.

Top British UFO experts were quick to back our discovery, but the Reds are already covering-up the incident.

''Unidentifiable organic molecular matter has been found in rocks before,'' said Arnold West, chairman of the British UFO Research Association.

RED SQUARE . . . where the sensational aliens story broke

monsters ARE landing on Earth...
ALL ALONG THEY'RE HERE!

AMAZING PHOTOGRAPHIC PROOF... of alien spacecraft hovering over the earth

"Of course, the Russians will never admit the significance of their find. Those rocks will probably never be seen again."

Although the Russian agency Tass initially reported the incident in detail, Kremlin bosses ordered a news black-out, after the rocks were discovered.

Frustrated Western journalists were met with a curt "Niet Commentski" as they tried to follow up the tale.

The only information available last night was that the aliens spoke FLUENT Russian!

Top Russian UFO investigator Vladimir Ruetave, who watched the Voronezh saucer drama unfold, said the sighting was of the SAME craft.

"It is quite extraordinary," said the 40-year-old sociology lecturer, who has made a special study of Soviet UFO sightings.

"These two incidents have happened thousands of miles apart, yet they appear to be atributable to the same spaceship."

Hatching the eggs

As the mystery deepened, it was revealed shell-shocked Soviet scientists have discovered the rocks left behind by the alien spaceship are ET eggs.

The baffled boffins are now trying to HATCH THEM at a secret space research centre deep in the Urals.

The amazing truth behind the extra-terrerstial landing was leaked to Sunday Sport investigators who rushed to Russia shortly after the sighting.

"The rocks appear to be pods which contain embryonic life," revealed a senior scientist working on the project.

"The embryos might be dead or just very slow growing, I can't say for certain at this time."

"We have only just started testing so it would be irresponsible to elaborate. But what we have discovered so far is UNIQUE."

Alien egg threat to world peace

■ THE ALIEN spaceship spotted in Russia and America may have launched an ET attempt at WORLD DOMINATION.

For incredibly, strange stones left behind by the aliens are now believed to be intergalactic EGGS — waiting to hatch!

■ "The fact the same craft has been spotted independently in both of the superpowers can only point to an invasion," warned one worried expert.

But last night the Russians staged an amazing about turn over the eggs scary secret.

■ The mystery rocks were first mentioned in Tass's announcement to the West.

Russian space offical Genrith Silanov said: "Mineralogical analysis has shown that the substance CANNOT be found on Earth."

■ But Silanov later changed his story after life forms were seen on X-ray plates and Commie bosses ordered a cover-up, phone operators pulling the plug on journalists.

JEALOUS HORSE SAYS: IT'S HER OR ME

Now Pete's saddled with love dilemma

Hay . . . can you two please stop horsing around, I wanna watch Neigh-bours!

THREE'S A CROWD . . . Albin with lovestruck Pete and girlfriend Sally

By SIMON FINLAY

LOVESTRUCK Pete Maier last night told how he pined for a stable relationship . . . so he moved in with a HORSE!

Potty Pete decided to share his home with piebald pony Albin, weeks after a chance meeting on a mountain.

But when Albin discovered the 39-year-old former clerk had a steady girlfriend, she became mulish and ruled: "It's either the bird of me!"

Naturally, Pete doesn't get his oats with frisky filly Albin — but he still reckons he's smitten.

"I love her. She's the best thing that has happened to me," he said.

The nag-lover added: "I was brought up in the city and longed to be able to run free like a horse in the country," said Pete, from Windischgarsten, Austria.

Then, one day in the Austrian mountains, the troubled bachelor spied the horse of his dreams.

It was love at first sight.

Responsive

"Horses are intelligent and very responsive to human affection," said Pete.

Then Albin discovered Pete had a serious girlfriend.

"I was absolutely bowled over when she met my girl Sally because Albin began rearing up and making very loud neighing noises," said Pete.

"She became incredibly possessive — to the point where she was prepared to be violent. I had to keep Sally away from the house because I couldn't bear to be parted from Albin," he added.

■ REGULARS at the Railway pub in Gorton, Manchester want to flush out the ghost of a former landlord called Jim who had a heart attack on the loo!

The spirit keeps using the toilet - and tampering with the jukebox and fruit machines.

SPACE ALIENS INVADING OUR KIDS' BRAINS

ARE YOU REALLY SOMEONE ELSE?

Elvis Express

ELVIS Presley is alive and well — and working, as a British Rail SIGNALMAN.

Wacky railway owner Peter Edwards from Ludlow, Shropshire, has changed his name by deed poll to live a bizarre life as the legendary rock and roll star.

Now he rides the Mystery Train and the Frankfurt Special.

Accent

He speaks with an American accent, wears specially tailored Elvis suits and even lives in a house called Gracelands.

"It means everything to me. I just love Elvis, I felt that the ultimate tribute would be to take his name," said Pete, 42.

"People just don't understand how I feel."

EVIL space aliens are INVADING children's minds in a NIGHTMARE to control the human race.

The sensational out-of-this-world revelation was made last night after one of the world's top psychologists tracked down a mini-army of ETs who are raiding the Earth to DESTROY US.

Now, in her Doomsday book called *Abductions**, Dr Edith Fiore has blown the lid on an intergalactic HOLOCAUST facing Mankind.

For more than 20 years, she has been hypnotising patients and probing their minds — with HORRIFYING results.

She claims her shocking interviews with alien invaders prove beyond doubt the world is on the BRINK of DESTRUCTION.

The petrified doctor, who is a practising clinical psychologist, is convinced SINISTER squads of ETs are taking over the minds of infants as their ageing bodies begin to die.

One of her many ALIEN

SPACE ALIENS invading kids' minds feel no remorse for their take-over. "It's our duty," one alien revealed when he went into a trance conducted by the worried doc. **SPOT**

By BILL CORKE

patients is Dan, a middle-aged American she hypnotised.

He told her he:

- **CAPTAINED** an invading spaceship
- **OBLITERATED** defenceless vitims, and
- **HELPED** plan a forthcoming invasion of Earth.

During his tape-recorded trance, Dan told Dr Fiore how he spent years scouring the galaxy in a heavily-armed Battlecruiser.

Memories

Frighteningly, the alien told how he came to Earth and assumed his new identity after taking over the body of a YOUNG BOY.

Dan says he selected his victim and took over all his memories.

"I have all his memories and all his patterns. My own memories will gradually fade."

On August 24 last year, Dan recalled, a Battlecruiser beamed him aboard for a reunion with his alien mates over Washington.

After a few drinks with the captain, Dan was transported back to Earth.

Describing the spacecraft, Dan said: "It was the same Battlecruiser I used to command. It's about a mile-and-a-half long and has a crew of 3,500.

"Each cruiser carries 14 smaller ships that can transport up to 100 people at a time."

*Abductions is published by Sidgwick & Jackson, London, price £13.95, from September.

SPACE SPACE folk enjoy a party, Dr Fiore has discovered. At least one alien left his craft on a takeover mission, the doctor has revealed, when they've been under the influence. **SPOT**

Smile wiped off superloo bosses

TAXMEN have pulled the chain on space age superloos by classing them as businesses. Councils have been caught with their pants down by having to pay up to 200 times more in rates.

SHOT AND CURLIES

HUBBY Greg Dickinson was shot by Indianapolis wife Karen in a row over who left a pubic hair on the toilet seat.

ET eggs rescued by our E-Team

Living dead's gonna get ya rants witch

ANGRY WITCH Barbara Brandolani last night issued a chilling warning to town hall bosses who want to demolish her home.

"All you will succeed in doing is unleashing a plague of DEMONS!"

The 50-year-old mother-of-seven claims there is a mass grave of PLAGUE VICTIMS beneath the basement of her historic home in Manchester.

And after housing bosses ruled the rundown former boatyard must be torn down before it falls down, Barbara said the dead will RISE and roam the city's streets

But a spokesman for Manchester City council stone-walled her protests.

"The house is in a very dangerous condition and we don't see any alternative to demolition," he said.

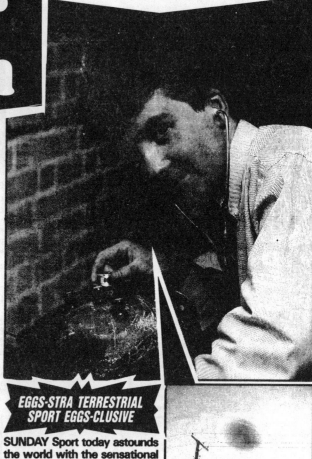

EGGS-STRA TERRESTRIAL SPORT EGGS-CLUSIVE

SUNDAY Sport today astounds the world with the sensational first-ever pictures of an ET EGG!

Our newsmen cracked tight security to rescue the unborn alien from the clutches of Soviet scientists.

Now the world's most forward-thinking newspaper will INCUBATE the outta-this-world egg and hatch the first CAPTIVE ET.

"I'm absolutely amazed by what you have done, this could be the most important scientific break through in history," one expert told Sunday Sport last night.

Now we intend bringing you weekly updates from our top-secret labs somewhere in Britain as we boldly go where no one has gone before — and attempt to rear an alien embryo.

We have a team of doctors on 24-hour stand-by to give whatever assistance they can at the historic moment when the ET breaks through its shell and enters our world.

Ultrasound scans show the tiny space baby bears an uncanny resemblance to a developing human embryo — but there are several vital differences.

It has an exceptionally small

By JON OGDEN

head and could have THREE eyes.

We jetted a team of newsmen to Russia as soon as news of confirmed sightings of alien landings at Voronezh were announced by the official Soviet news agency TASS.

Our newsmen swung into action to stop Commie boffins carrying out experiments on the ET eggs in SECRET.

The resourceful reporters spirited them from behind the Iron Curtain by hiding them in a carrier bag between duty free

EGGS-AMINATION ... reporter Ogden gives the alien egg the once-over and (above) from last week's Sunday Sport.

bottles of vodka.

UFO expert Elsie Lee said: "Four years ago, a story came out that a spaceship crashed in Russia — but an infant survived in an escape capsule.

"Scientists were able to keep it alive for four days before it succumbed to an infection," added Elsie at her home in Chesterfield, Derbyshire.

● The ETA — estimated time of arrival — of the baby alien is five weeks from today.

Cat licks junk habit

A JUNKIE cat whose heartless owner shot him up with dope has finally kicked the habit.

Worried neighbours alerted animal welfare workers after they saw Stuffy the cat staggering around stoned.

The seven-year-old puss was rescued from his addict owner in Lauwreszijl, Holland, and given barbituates to wean him off the drug.

Now the reformed moggy is fit, and back on cat food — from the bowl.

Pompey John's winning name

CRAZY Pompey fan John Westwood has made his LOVE for the club legal.

He is now officially known as John Anthony Portsmouth Football Club Westwood.

John, 26, paid £30 to register the formal declaration.

He said: "I love the club and I haven't missed a game, for eight years."

UFO COPS IN CAR CHASE

AMAZED motorists last night told how a UFO cop car chased them along a road!

"We noticed a large blue light blinking on and off overhead," said driver Alan Shaehan, of Portland, Australia.

"It looked like the beacon on a patrol car. But it was much brighter.

"As we watched the UFO flew horizontally out to sea!"

Terrified tourists' monster shocker

By BILL PEARCE

TERRIFIED tourists fled in fear after a baby monster raised its house-high head from Britain's largest lake, it was revealed last night.

The sea serpent in Lake Windermere, Cumbria, is believed to be the offspring of the famed Loch Ness Monster, which is some 150 miles away.

Startled weekend tripper Maria Taylor from Manchester said: "It was absolutely hideous. I went for a moonlight stroll round the lake, and saw him bobbing over the waves.

Dreadful

"He was huge, and scared the life out of me. *A gang of lads came running when he let out a dreadful shriek. We all stood on the floor quaking.*"

A local told Marie there had been numerous sightings of the monster — and they had dubbed him the Bowness Monster after a lakeside resort.

HUNGRY TOMATO WANTED ME FOR DINNER!

By Our Gardening Correspondent ANDY HARRIS

TERRIFIED builder Eric Crombie shocked gardening experts yesterday... by claiming he was chased off an allotment by a KILLER TOMATO.

Stunned Eric says he was forced to run for his life when the snarling salad-ball sprouted legs and tried to EAT him for dinner.

And as the 15-stone father-of-two was recovering at home last night, green-fingered boffins warned Britain could be facing an onslaught from MUTANT VEGETABLES.

"I know people will think I'm joking but I know what I saw," quaked Eric.

Balloon

"I looked out of the window and saw this huge red ball — it must have been at least four foot wide," he revealed.

"It let out this horrible snarl, sprouted limbs and started running towards me on all fours," he claimed.

"I've never been so terrified in my life — I took one look at it and ran."

Now Eric is REFUSING to return to his allotment near Stoke-on-Trent until the soil is examined by scientists.

"I've read about fall-out from Chernobyl — the Russian nuclear disaster — causing things to mutate. For all we know this could be the start of an epidemic," he claimed.

RED-FACED... Eric

Experts believe the killer tomato could be the work of a deranged botanist.

"Gardening has now become so scientific that almost anything can be done to increase of decrease the size of a fruit or vegetable," confirmed Kew Gardens David Ray.

COP FOR A BABY

CLEVER cop Andrea Byron didn't know where to turn when a heavily preggers mum turned up at Tottenham police station, in north London, but she helped deliver a 6lb boy

---

Mad bull has wife bog-eyed

TERRIFIED housewife Barbara Deck last night told how she was caught short — when an angry BULL crashed through a toilet wall!

"I was scared stiff. I couldn't move. The bull looked me straight in the eye and came at me," she told an astonished courtroom.

Horns

In a desperate bid to save her life, brave Babs grabbed the beast by the horns and wrestled with it for two minutes until help arrived, with her knickers round her ankles.

But the incident, at a North Dakota rodeo, left her with a badly bruised back. She was awarded £10,000 damages, and an apology from rodeo organisers.

Bertie bullock takes flight...

WIDE–EYED birdwatchers were in a FLAP last night after they were buzzed... by Bertie the flying BULLOCK!

They looked on in amazement as Bertie slipped over a 40ft cliff and had to be rescued by an RAF helicopter crew.

A chopper from 202 Search and Rescue Squadron based at Brawdy was scrambled after RSPCA men failed to hoist the beast to safety.

They dropped a net around Bertie and airlifted him to safety at St Govan's Head, Dyfed, Wales.

"It was a useful training exercise and we suspect Bertie was mightily relieved as well," said spokesman David Pengilly.

TALKING TEA-POT LETS OFF STEAM

LABOUR LEADER HAUNTED BY POTTY GHOST!

LABOUR leader Neil Kinnock was given the biggest roasting of his political life last night... by a TALKING TEAPOT!

The fiery MP — cruelly dubbed the Welsh Windbag by parliamentary enemies — got a scalding when the prattling pot spouted off, and began BARKING orders to him.

Last night, stunned pot-owner John Craft said the teapot is being HAUNTED by the ghost of former Labour big-shot Nye Bevan.

Frightened John said: "I was about to make my morning cuppa when I heard this strange rattling noise coming from the pot.

"It got louder and louder — and then I heard this squeaky little voice coming from the spout. It sounded very angry and kept on about the state of the nation and the NHS."

John, 22, a painter from

END IS NYE... John, right, and Matthew

By JOHN GARVEY

Warwick, said: "Just the other night it kept repeating the name Neil Kinnock over and over.

"It was trying to give him instructions."

John said he was baffled until he called a friend — keen local historian Matthew Geden.

Matthew said: "I heard the voice, too, and recognised Bevan's style at once. I played colleagues a tape and they confirmed my findings. But I have no logical explanation."

A spokesman for Labour Leader Neil Kinnock said last night: "Mr Kinnock is on holiday in Italy at the moment.

"But it may be significant that he is a great admirer of Nye Bevan. He even wrote the introduction to the Penguin edition of Nye's book, In Place of Fear."

John is now trying to make a transcript of the ghostly messages to send to the Labour boss. But he misses his cuppa. He said: "I can't bring myself to pour boiling water on Nye."

GOBBLIN' TURKEY TRIED TO STUFF ME

By gobblesmacked BRANDON MALINSKY

A GIANT killer turkey was on the loose last night...after trying to STUFF its owner.

The FOUR-FOOT tall monster went CRACKERS and launched a frenzied attack on gobble smacked Mark Sutton as he fed it in his garden.

"At one stage it picked me up by the legs and tried to stuff me with a couple of GROW-BAGS," he admitted last night.

"I clenched my cheeks together and somehow managed to fight my way free."

Brave Mark, 31, showed he wasn't CHICKEN by standing up to the barmy bird.

But yesterday he warned: "Please stay away from that turkey. It'll make a meal of you!"

Derby miner Mark added: "It's made a right mess of my face and body, but the mental scars will be most difficult to get rid of.

"It was like a weird

VICTIM ... Mark

REVENGE for the millions of turkeys that bite the dust every Christmas."

Mark, who bred the turkey spcially for Christmas was chased into his house and had to bolt the door to keep out the FEATHERED FIEND.

When he PLUCKED up COURAGE to look outside, the runaway turkey was dashing across a nearby golf course.

'I suppose it attacked me when it realised it was for the chop," said Mark.

Loving

"It was going to be the best Christmas nosh ever. I'd have needed a van full of Paxo to stuff the bugger.

"I nurtured it with loving care from an egg. It was fed on a concoction which my mate uses to grow giant leeks," he added.

Points win for scrumdown girls

THE Welsh women's rugby squad aims to be out in front ... thanks to a new BOOB protector invented by coach Jeff Williams' wife June to protect the girl's whoppas.

Rampant sheep attack islanders

VICTIMS of sheep attacks in New Zealand last year claimed thousands of pounds in recompense.

The Accident Compensation Corporation say 678 people were bitten or rammed.

N.A.S.A. PLANS SPACE JOKER

By GAZZA THOMPSON

HOLY SPACEPLOT! NASA bosses have come up with a bizarre plan to rake in the dollars . . . they want to blast The Joker into ORBIT!

Space experts reckon actor Jack Nicholson—who plays Batman's arch-rival in the big screen smash—is the ideal all-American idol to head their latest publicity campaign.

And NASA insiders have revealed they've already got the space-wagon rolling by approaching the star with the offer of pioneering a celebrity space shuttle flight.

Their amazing package includes:

● **POW!** A no-expense spared training programme that will see Nicholson undergo zero gravity work-outs.

● **WHAM!** A multi-million pound contract with Nicholson almost certainly being offered the chance to play himself in a movie dramatisation of the stunt.

● **KRUNCH!** A controlled spacewalk to be broadcast live on television throughout the West.

"In effect we'll be sending a star among the stars," confided one NASA source quoted in a leading American newspaper.

"Mr. Nicholson will get the experience of a lifetime and we'll reap a publicity windfall from the fans and the public."

Space bosses believe the stunt will help them win back funds and public support which suffered badly after the 1986 shuttle disaster.

Influence

"The project should influence Congress and help us get the additional funding we desperately need to speed up space exploration," added the NASA insider.

The star's Los Angeles-based management company are making no official comment on the deal but Nicholson is believed to be flattered by the offer.

LOCH MONS

CAPTURED ON FILM . . .

NAZI

NESS
STER IS

the sneaky submarine breaks the surface of Loch Ness on its monster mission

U-BOAT

EXCLUSIVE

MILITARY officials were baffled last night after the Loch Ness monster was sensationally exposed... as a Nazi U-BOAT!

This amazing photograph

● CONTINUED ON PAGE 7

MAKING WAVES . . . *these amazing pictures of what was thought to be Nessie have fooled the world for years. Now your ever-vigilant Sunday Sport has exposed the truth*

NESSIE SECRET EXPOSED... IT'S A NAZI U-BOAT

A SEARCH was launched last night for the Loch Ness submarine and its mystery crew.

Boffins have demanded the DREDGING of the lake, to uncover — once and for all — its amazing secrets.

The U-boat pictures — snapped by an innocent holidaymaker — have fuelled speculation that Germany was planning to INVADE Scotland.

And with a Nazi boat spotted in the loch just TWO WEEKS AGO, fears have grown that the war may not be over YET!

REAL NESSIE . . . *no bulging eyes — just a periscope, but the threat from this monster could be very real indeed*

■ LOCH Ness is the largest lake in Britain — more than 22 miles long — and the third deepest in Europe at 975ft.

As well as the ''monster'', it is home to salmon, trout, char and eels. Neighbours include red deer, golden eagles, wildcats and lots of Gaelic-speaking Scotsmen. Nessie's home is rainy and cold — but locals wouldn't swop it for the world.

Historians were trying to work out how and why a German U-boat emerged in the lake exactly 50 years AFTER the war.

They want to know:
● HOW the crew have survived;
● WHERE are they now; and
● DO they realise the war is over?

Experts say the U-boat discovery could be the answer to one of the biggest mysteries north of the border.

It may solve the riddle of why Rudolf Hess, the deputy Führer, mysteriously parachuted into Scotland in 1941.

''Ostensibly, it was to try to bring about peace between Britain and Germany,'' said historian Tony Charman.

''At the time, Hess was being pushed into the background while generals like Goering were achieving prominence.

''This was a way of re-establishing himself with Hitler. Hess was in a strange mental condition.

''One will never know exactly what happened.''

The sub could also mean that Hitler had long planned to invade from the NORTH!

The Führer knew all Britain was on alert against an invasion force arriving by sea or air.

Choosing Scotland as a landing point for the invasion of Britain would have caught Churchill completely off guard, Hitler knew, because everyone expected the Hun to attack via the Channel.

''The invasion plans were thought to be almost exclusively on the south coast of England,'' confirmed historian Tony.

The boat could have entered Loch Ness through a natural channel from the open sea of the Moray Firth — just six miles away.

''It's possible there's a geological loch between the loch and the sea,'' said Colin Kirkland, President of the International Tunnelling Association and Technical Director of Eurotunnel.

Sub in Ness to save Hess

VISITOR . . . Hess

● **FROM PAGE 1**
has sparked incredible speculation that the crew is STILL ALIVE.

''The total number of U-boats lost in the war was 785 but 29 of those were listed as vanishing for UNKNOWN CAUSES,'' revealed a spokesman for the Imperial War Museum in London.

''No one knows what happened to them — even now, 50 years after the war there are still facts coming to light that at the time were swept under the carpet.''

Now villagers around Loch Ness are CONVINCED one of the missing subs is the solution to hundreds of ''Nessie'' sightings.

''I did once hear a local saying there was a submarine in Loch Ness,'' revealed landlord Dave Moffat, who runs the Dores Inn, next to the Loch.

''A German U-boat certainly penetrated the naval base at nearby Cromarty during the war.''

Our amazing front page photograph was taken two weeks ago by a wealthy American tourist — who asked Sunday Sport to keep his identity secret.

''The sub was only on the surface for a few minutes but I saw it clearly,'' he revealed.

''Afterwards I thought I must have imagined it and kept quiet.''

Now people believe the U-boat may have been sent to Scotland to rescue Rudolf Hess.

GOTCHA!

U-BOAT commander Hans von Munchhausen has emerged from his submarine in Loch Ness . . . to SURRENDER!

Fifty years after the war, the Kraut captain has finally agreed to admit defeat.

He asked Sunday Sport: "Show me where to find Mr Churchill — I want to tell him he's won."

Captain Hans was in command of a German U-boat on a top secret mission in the famous Scottish lake.

His orders were to sneak into

HANS UP . . . U-boat boss Hans and Iron Cross record

Ve hav vays ov makin' 'im talk to us . . .

By DOMINIC KENNEDY

Loch Ness and remain there unseen until further instructions were received from Hitler.

But when the Sunday Sport exclusively published a picture of the U-boat two weeks ago, Hans knew the game was up.

He said: "One of the crew had slipped ashore and came back clutching a copy of your paper.

Message

"The men couldn't believe it when we realised the war must be over — and the Fuhrer was dead.

"We were still waiting for a radio message from Berlin — the last time we heard anything was 1944.

"I can't remember the exact date, but I'm pretty sure it was a Tuesday."

Captain Hans, 65, said his 50-man crew were all in their twenties when they arrived in Loch Ness.

Now the old seadogs want to go home to the Fatherland and collect their war pensions.

It'll be a great relief to get off that bloody U-boat," he said.

"All we've had is FISH for tea EVERY NIGHT for 50 years.

We've got a gramophone on baord, but we only brought along two records — Lili Marlene and It's A Long Way To Tipperary.

"We didn't even see the schweinhund monster!"

FLAMING JAMMY GHOSTBUSTER

GOBSMACKED ghostbusters were in a spin last night, after a top boffin claimed sweet-toothed spirits can be caught in JAM JARS!

Scientists studying the paranormal were told to dump their high-tech tools.

For potty Prof Jozef Kaposi has perfected a bizarre, DIY method of grabbing the GHOSTIES by the GHOULIES!

All you need is a jam jar and candle.

The nutty Hungarian parapsychology expert said: "Nobody knows why, but a ghost can't resist traces of jam left in the container.

"Once inside, the energy from the burning candle will trap it."

Prof Kaposi said once the lid

OUR STORIES PUT YOU IN HIGH SPIRITS

By JOHN GARVEY

screwed shut, the spirit is trapped for eternity — or until the glass is broken.

Prof Kaposi perfected his method after being called to a HAUNTING in Budapest, Hungary.

He said: "A strange, glowing shape appeared, and seemed attracted to a jam pot which had not been properly secured.

"It is an established fact burning candles trap ghosts, so I just put two and two together."

Prof Kaposi added: "It sounds far-fetched, but catching a spirit is SIMPLE.

"I have used the technique to capture half a dozen ghosts, which proves my method works. It is safe and effective.

"Ghosts are a natural phenomenon and can be dispensed with naturally."

Prof Kaposi's claims SHOCKED top British

ghostbuster, psychologist *Robin Furman.*

He and his team of scientists offer a ghostbusting service using the latest, state-of-the-art equipment — including lasers and computers.

Mr Furman said: "I have no evidence that Professor Kaposi's method does NOT work. But it's unlikely.

"Most ghosts aren't really ghosts, in the accepted sense of the word, but images of the past replayed like a film."

SPOOKY . . . Prof Kaposi

BIRD S*!* CURED MY BALDNESS!

...Bum fluff sprouts after pigeon parcel

HAIRS *Joe's bum fluff*

By BERTIE OLLOCKS

EX-CHROME DOME Joe Dunn stuck a feather in his cap last night to celebrate his miracle cure for baldness — PIGEON SH*T!

The incredible remedy hit him six months ago — when a parcel from a pigeon's bum splattered his pate.

A few weeks later he was AMAZED to discover HAIR sprouting from the spot where it hit.

PROOF *Before the splat*

Now Joe hopes to cash in on his hair-raising experience by BOTTLING the stuff and flogging it to fellow baldies under the name EXCRETION 2000!

Joe, 56, of Milton, Stoke-on-Trent, said: "I could hardly believe it. The new growth was THICK and STRONG.

"*The next problem was how to get other pigeons to cr*p on my head.*"

Smeared

He hit on the answer when he came across an old friend who kept pigeons.

Joe said: "I persuaded him to let me go into his loft and I lay down and closed my eyes.

"Within half an hour, I was PLASTERED in the stuff and I smeared it into my scalp."

For the next few days, the PONG of pigeon sh*t was OVERPOWERING.

But he persevered and, within a month, was rewarded with a new head of healthy hair.

Axe-tually, I've got a splitting headache

STUNNED doctors stared in disbelief when Dick Collins strolled into a surgery with a headache . . . and an AXE-blade buried in his BRAINS.

But the wacky woodcutter calmly told docs not to worry — it had been there for 52 YEARS!

Dick was whisked to hospital, where surgeons performed a delecate operation to remove the blade.

Dick explained that it lodged in his skull in 1937, when a fellow woodcutter's blake flew from his axe.

He left it there despite blinding headaches. But finally the pain became too much, and Dick, of Port Elizabeth, South Africa, sought help.

Dr Edwin Deare, who removed the axe, said last night: "By rights, he should be long dead."

Worms hook 'em

SHAKEN but not stirred Yank tipplers love the crunchy bite of juicy worm swimming in their fluted glasses.

Some trendy bars even stock a worm tank for fresh pickings — filled with rich soil and loaded with wriggly, squiggly worms.

FAT DOG TURNS INTO A PIG

Sizzling Pictures
Page 4

Pet pooch pinched by Satan's sweeper

A HORRIFIED housewife swears a Hoover from Hell sucked up her pet poddle and swallowed him whole!

And she's convinced the Devil is living INSIDE the innocent-looking vacuum cleaner.

Birgitta Himmelstein is now terrified the horror Hoover might attack her and her husband Ludwig.

"There was nothing I could do," she wept as she relived the shocking moment the carpet cleaner lunged out of her hands and raced towards the sleeping pooch, Elmo.

"It rolled right on top of him and made a horrible sucking sound. Elmo yelped but his head got sucked into the bag and was suffocated.

"I know that vacuum cleaner's posssessed and the Devil will get me if I touch it," said Birgitta, of Flensburg, West Germany.

Hot stuff

A revenous rat started a fire at Vera Bell's Northumberland home, by eating a box of matches and igniting them.

White night's Bill's delight

BATTY biologist Bill McKibben wants to turn the sky WHITE to save the earth from the GREENhouse effect.

Bill says millions of tons of sulphur dioxide gas will protect us from the sun's rays.

DOGWASH —IT'S A PIG

PEEKIN' EASY . . . a real Shar-pei dog

HOGSMACKED pensioners Willie and Margarete Decker are suing a top breeder for £65,000 . . . because their prize pooch is a PIG!

The couple went BARKING MAD when they took the animal to a Crufts-style show and were told by judges: "You must be doggone joking!"

Now they've taken legal action alleging breeder Harry Bartels told a PORKY PIE and sold them a £500 boar which looks like a pedigree £3,000 Chinese Shar-Pei dog.

"I've never been so humiliated in my life," said furious Willie, 73.

"My wife and I took him to a dog show, expecting to win first prize.

"But the judges took one look at him and threw us out. They said 'That's no dog. That's a PIG!'

"They acted like we were out of our minds."

Amazingly, the pensioners didn't sniff out the truth when they got the porker home.

And the happy hog was so friendly, Willie and Margarete named him Sweetie.

"I'd like to keep him, if

Fat's life . . . amazed couple get porka shocka

it wasn't for the cost and embarrassment," said Margarete, 71.

"At the moment, we are a laughing stock. Everybody thinks we're just a pair of senile fuddy-duddies because we can't tell a pig from a dog."

The Deckers' lawyer, Peter Nolte, alleges Bartels changed registration documents so it looked like the pig came from a line of champion dogs.

"He was full-grown when they bought him and Bartels allegedly told them they could earn £6,500 a year in stud fees alone," said Mr Nolte.

In their lawsuit, Willie and Margarete, from Baden-Baden, West Germany, are claiming compensation for "humiliation and mental anguish".

The pig — a Meishan — is bred in China, as are Shar-Pei dogs.

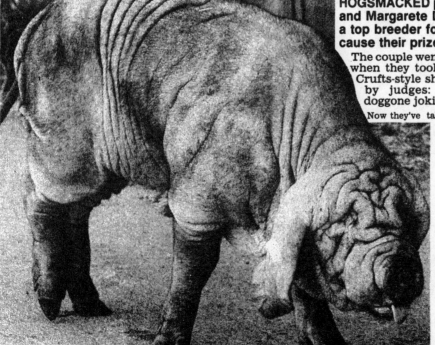

PORKER . . . the 'superior' hog sold to the puzzled pensioners

PIECES OF ATE

CAT GOBBLES PARROT...AND TALKS!

By Veterinary Reporter JOHN GARVEY

BENJI the black and white tom cat stunned the science world last night after he guzzled a parrot... and started **TALKING!**

His shocked owner, glazier Chris Morris, was sickened at first when he returned home to find a pile of bloody feathers on the floor beside Percy the parrot's empty cage.'

But his horror turned to amazement when Benji licked his lips greedily, opened his mouth — and SPOKE.

With a trembling hand, Chris poured himself a large scotch, sat back in his chair and waited.

Toying nervously with Percy's favourite piece of cuttlefish on which he sharpened his beak, Chris said last night: "I was shaken to the core.

"It started out as this strange mewing sound, but gradually started to form words."

Chris, 26, added: "As I listened, I gradually became able to make out words.

"I heard Benji say: 'Percy wants a cracker.' I kept quiet about it because I thought people would think I was crazy."

But Benjie's bizarre ability became obvious when friends dropped round and were astonished to hear the cat forming words.

Logical

Chris, of Baddely Green, Stoke-on-Trent, said: "It's absolutely astonishing.

"No-one who has heard it can believe their ears. I can think of no logical explanation."

Animal psychologist Dr Trevor Hammond said last night: "Ther is nothing in the physical make-up of a cat's vocal chords to prevent them talking.

"It's just that they don't have the intelligence."

And Victor Watkins, a spokesman for the Royal Society for the Protection of Animals, said: "This is truly remarkable."

Benji was unavailable for comment when our reporter telephoned his home last night. *Gobsmacked glazier Chris revealed he has been snowed*

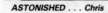

under with calls from science journals and psychics since news of his pet's incredible ability leaked out.

But he said: "I've had enough. I hear that nine out of ten cats prefer Whiskas.

"It's just my luck to have the one that prefers PARROTS."

● Benji's bizarre case is not unique.

Last month we exclusively revealed how painter John Craft was stunned when his TEAPOT talked to him.

Experts in paranormal research revealed the prattling pot was haunted by the ghost of former Labour firebrand Aneurin Bevan after it began barking orders at Neil Kinnock!

BIZARRE . . . Benji

ASTONISHED . . . Chris

Tony . . . gasping

Killer prawn!

HERO ex-cop Wilf Knight told last night how he saved hunky Bill actor Tony Scannell from choking to death . . . on a KING PRAWN!

Telly heart-throb Tony —who plays tough-guy Ted Roach in the smash ITV series—was purple-faced and gasping for air until Wilf dived to the rescue.

Tony had been sitting alone in the canteen at The Bill's studios in West London when his prawn curry caught in the back of his throat.

Plucky Wilf, police adviser to the series, put pressure on his diaphragm to save his life— and the prawn popped out.

PSYCHIC SPROG SENDS EGGHEADS GAGA

Mum's snap traps spirit

Tunna money for wife hit by flying fish!

By BERTIE OLLOCKS

PROOF . . . of toddler's ghostly pal

HOUSEWIFE Dorothy Lonsdale has sent the science world potty . . . by claiming she's the proud mum of Britain's first ever PSYCHIC SPROG !

For, incredibly, little Vicky Lonsdale has rattled her family by gurgling in baby-talk to a POLTERGEIST.

And last night mum Dorothy stunned paranormal researchers by announcing she's captured the amazing mite and her goo-goo ghost pal ON FILM.

Wherever she goes, weird noises surround Vicki and heavy ornaments move mysteriously.

Mystified mum, Dorothy said: "Ever since she was a baby, I noticed strange noises in the house, footsteps and voices.

"I'm not superstitious, so I used to ignore these things."

Weird

The worried mum was finally convinced something weird was going on when she developed a film taken on Vicky's second birthday.

Her daughter was splashing in the bath . . . and staring happily up at a strange, ghostly white shape.

Dorothy, of Paignton, Devon, said: "A photographer friend of mine studied the photo and said it was very, very strange. It was not a reflection of the flash, or anything like that."

A College for Psychic Research spokesman said: "Obviously she is a very psychic little girl."

A WOMAN who was walloped by a frozen FISH during a tuna-tossing contest has won £20,000 damages.

Stunned Sharon Szabo, 37, was smacked in the back during the fish flinging contest in Port Lincoln, Australia.

Her husband Mark says she STILL suffers back pains after the rock-hard fish was included in the contest by mistake.

Funny

"It sounds funny, but it has not been a happy time for us," said Mark, 42.

"My wife can't hang out the washing or vacuum without pain."

Fish flinging—in which the contestant throws a fully grown tuna attached to a steel hook down a grass course—is a growing cult down under.

Pieces o' fight!

A FEATHER-BRAINED thief who nicked a £500 mynah bird ditched it . . . because it's a Millwall supporter.

The bird - which squawks the name of the fearsome team - was found dumped soon after being nicked from a shop in Hendon, North London.

A police spokesman joked:"Unfortunately it refused to sing like a bird and give us some leads on the thief."

RAF PILOTS' PLEA TO SEARCH FOR

Fares keep a lonely vigil at the Pole

SUNDAY SPORT

BUS

Polar trip put on ice 'cos fare's too much!

AIR FORCE bigwigs last night made a sensational plea to rescue the famous London double-decker bus found at the South Pole.

But the high flyers have been told to GROUND a secret flight to save the stricken Number 109 — revealed on Sunday Sport's front page on February 12 this year.

The world was stunned when we told how the bus pulled out of a garage in Croydon, Surrey, only to be found buried up to its front axle in a glacier.

Shocked pilots and navigators at RAF Lyneham, Wilts, were told five months ago to prepare for the hush-hush raid on the ice-cap.

The elite task-force was even ordered to go to remote regions of Canada and Alaska to train for an airlift in freezing temperatures in an operation costing an incredible £10 MILLION.

But in an astonishing about-face, the team was told the mission was to be SCRAPPED by the Government because the price was too HIGH.

And a spokeswoman for the Ministry of Defence ADMITTED the exercise

By SIMON FINLAY

would be TOO COSTLY.

"We have an annual budget of £20,143 million this year. An operation to the South Pole of this nature would not be economically sensible," said the MoD's Sheila Thompson.

But RAF men were OUTRAGED by the waste of cash in the preparations for the rescue.

Appalling

One stunned navigator admitted: "I'm stunned and appalled they've pulled out now.

"We were told we would airlift the bus to a waiting carrier ship which would transport it back to England for tests," he added.

Military experts last night CONFIRMED the RAF is capable of carrying out the incredible mission.

"I would imagine it is possible. After all, the RAF operate in the Falklands as well as Canada and have the sort of lifting gear they would need," said Ian Geldard of the respected military magazine Terror Update.

Heavens! How to end a dog's life

A PSYCHIC healer wants deceased pooches to be given a full Christian burial.

Spiritualist Clive Garnett, who cures pets by laying on hands and is a practising Christian, believes animal souls come back to haunt their earthly owners.

Clive, 54, whose technique has cured hundreds of dogs, cats, birds and horses, trained at theological college.

Dignity

" Animals survive death just like us and it is important they are not just buried in a hole in the ground —they should be treated with dignity and respect," said Portsmouth-based Clive.

Clive, who has started to give unofficial burials to pets, added : " I know people who have seen, felt and heard their pets after they have died."

" They are God-given too and should be treated with reverence."

Tomato fever fiend blasted

A VEG-mad pensioner was shot in the mouth . . . because he had a TOMATO frenzy!

"Richard Dieppe told brother Clarence to stop poking around in the refrigerator, looking for tomatoes", said the Sherrif's department in La Motto, Iona.

"He then got a .22 pistol and fired a shot, striking Clarence in the cheek area."

TRAGIC pensioner Douglas Cooper died after trying to get a ration of rumpy-pumpy, an inquest heard.

For the 70-year-old OAP ignored doctor's orders and had an operation to cure his impotence.

Randy Douglas persuaded medics to treat him for his embarrassing problem — because he didn't want to die without a BONK.

He told doctors: "I've only got two or three years left — and I want to make the most of them!"

But the retired architect's heart was too weak to withstand the gruelling operation.

Gruelling

GP Dr David Spraggett told the Birmingham inquest that his patient had a history of heart disease.

"He was very worried about his impotence and came to me for treatment. At first he was given injections and then an operation was suggested," said Dr Spraggett.

Urologist Dr Clive Young took over the pensioner's case and carried out the op at Selly Oak Hospital, Birmingham.

Dr Young warned Douglas about the risks of the anaesthetic because of his heart condition.

Then the architect wrote Dr Young a letter stating: "I am now 70 and statistically I have only two or three years of life left. I know the risks and want to go ahead."

Verdict: Natural causes.

PORK OFF! PIG-LOVER GETS HER TROTTIN' ORDERS!

PET-CRAZY teenager Grace Sarker has been given her marching orders... for living with a PIG.

Animal-lover Grace has quit her bedsit after landlady Khaleda Choudhury told her it was a no-go zone for porkers.

Grace refused to part with the friendly squealer and insisted: "It's just like having a baby in the house."

As if to prove her point, Grace treats her 13-week-old porker, Moses, as though it were a toddler by:

● BATHING the piglet twice a week;

● FEEDING him small portions of her OWN food;

● WALKING the squealer three times a day;

● TUCKING Moses up every night in his very own COT.

"When I first got Moses, I wondered what I'd taken on," she confessed.

"But now I'm used to him. He's just like a baby — and a lot better than a dog.

Grace, a former student at the London Studio Centre, took Moses into her tiny bedsit to save him from the slaughterhouse.

"I read about what happened to pigs before they're slaughtered, so I decided to go and get one and keep it," she said.

"A lot of people think pigs are really dirty animals, but they're not.

"When I take him out for walks, I do get a few strange looks," said the

SQUEAL APPEAL... Grace and pig

By PHIL MILLAN

cheery teenager, who's now staying with friends in Wales.

"The children really love him. They stop and talk and try to stroke him.

Celebrity

Neighbour Alan Robinson, 42, said: "Grace is a lovely girl and she obviously loves the pig very much.

"She takes it for walks all over Arsenal on a leash. She is becoming a bit of a local celebrity.

"There was never any trouble with the RSPCA or the police — it's her landlady who's not too keen."

Landlady Khaleda Choudhury stormed: "Nobody in their right mind could let a pig stay in their room — the whole house was getting smelly.

"She'd already arranged to move out. But if she'd have wanted to stay with the pig I certainly wouldn't have let her."

Granny shaken by cure

BLIND granny Eleanor got her eyesight back after being shaken by a powerful EARTHQUAKE!

Eleanor Gibbs, 72, thought she was dreaming when her sight was magically restored when the tremors passed after 30 seconds.

Opened

"It was like a miracle," said Eleanor, from Newcastle, Australia.

"I felt like my eyes were being opened for the first time in years. I went outside and I could see everything as plain as day.

"I can now see my grandchildren properly. My sight was going for years and completely failed two years ago—but now it is back," she added.

Creepy-crawly pets for Japs

BUG-BARMY Japs are forking out an incredible £550 for creepy-crawlies . . . to keep as household PETS!

For the insect-mad Orientals are prepared to dish the dosh for a rare species like the Stag Beetle.

"The Japanese love nature and bugs are part of nature," said Mariko Gibbons — a collector.

"Kids buy cheaper bugs but some adults pay a lot of money for sought-after species."

Monster deep sea terror

FOURTEEN passengers and crew were forced to swim for their lives after their boat was sunk by a GIANT OCTOPUS!

And boat skipper Ele Sarino reckons the slimy creature wanted revenge.

"I remembered the thousands of octopuses I'd caught and I thought 'Here comes their great-grandfather — he's after revenge'!" said Ele.

The beast's eight feet long tentacles capsized the vessel off the Phillipines coast.

JILTED RAINMAN IN STORM OVER LOVER

■ Cascade for Casca . . . the wacky weatherman claims he can bring on rain-damage with his mental powers.

JILTED rainmaker Casca Crowley last night told how he got even with his estranged lover . . . by starting a thunderstorm over her head.

For the fuming council worker claims he can change the weather by simply looking at the sky.

And he reckoned that would be the best way to stop blonde Maria Bellingham from meeting her new fella. But it was a washout.

"I just wanted a little downpour so she would have to cancel her date. I didn't mean

By SIMON FINLAY

it to rain solidly for four days," said 24-year-old Casca at his Leicester home.

"In the end, I had to do a special gyrating, wriggling dance on top of a hill to get it to stop."

Casca took revenge on Maria after she told him she was leaving him for another guy.

"She told me she was going to meet him that night, but I told

her I could stop her by changing the weather," said Casca.

"I went outside and zapped my MENTAL VIBES at the sky and directed a thunderstorm above her. It worked.

The wacky weatherman says his bizarre power stems from Buddhism. But he said: "I'm not into religion — I have a gift."

● If YOU want to witness Casca's incredible rainmaking skills, write to him c/o *Sunday Sport, Marten House, 39-47 East Road, London N1 7AH*, and we'll pass your letters on.

MISSUS TELLS BOGEY LOVER TO... FLICK OFF!

● ROGER

IT'S SNOT ON SAYS BUTCHER WIFE

By GAZZA THOMPSON

TRUCK driver Roger Deaton was at the centre of a bizarre love triangle last night . . . torn between his missus and a giant green BOGEY!

Nutty Roger fell in love with the shapely lump of snot called Grollie, who's grown to the size of a GOLFBALL.

But his jealous girlfriend, Tracey Wellings, 23, turned GREEN with ENVY and told him: "You can flick off. It's me or the bogey."

Now Roger, 27, faces an agonising choice. He moaned: "It's just SNOT fair."

He added: "I began collecting my bogeys two years ago and roll them into one big ball — now it's HUGE.

"I suppose I was bored and needed a hobby.

I had a nose full of them all the time and I couldn't think why I was throwing them away.

"People I know wipe them under the chair or eat them. I thought I would keep them."

Cracking

"I have to spray HER every morning to stop her dehydrating and cracking.

"It'll break my heart to see her go, she's lovely," added the Royal Mail driver.

Grollie takes pride of place on the bedside table at his home in Luton, Beds.

"First thing in the morning and last thing at night is the best time for picking bogeys and getting some dust in the cab is great. It means I get more."

But Tracey — a butcher — is determined to give her rival the CHOP.

She said: "His hobby is DISGUSTING. Would you like it if your lover had been collecting snot? He's got to stop."

Loo-ser Andy wipes off his parking fines

By KIZZI NKWOCHA

WACKY whizz kid Andy McIntosh thought cops were BUMS for giving him a load of parking tickets so he wrote them a cheque . . . on a LOO!

BOG-SMACKED Andy, 25, sent in his kami-khazi caper after picking up nine tickets outside his East Croydon home since May.

Furious Andy, who says his bizarre cheque is legal, has started his own group called CRAP — Croydon Residents' Against Parking tickets — to help fight fines. "I think it's bang out of order I can't park outside my own door," he fumed.

"First I POO-POO'd the fines and wrote out cheques on BOG ROLL but got tired of doing that.

"I guess you could call me twisted, but I remembered a mate of mine is a plumber so I went to see him and he gave me the loo. I thought, 'wait' till they WC that'!

"I delivered it personally and I checked with the bank to make sure it's legal."

But his LOO-DICROUS stunt has left traffic cops FLUSHED with anger!

Payment

"We were NOT amused," said a spokesman for the Metropolitan Police Fixed Penalty Office.

"We're trying to run an office as efficiently as we can and this is a big INCONVENIENCE — but I expect it's better than just getting the toilet in LOO of payment."

Now ex-banker Andy, who works as a financial consultant, says he's already got a dozen members for his group.

"I want everyone to join in this campaign," he said.

"We're going to get our parking fines together and fight them with CRAP."

LOO-DICROUS . . . angry Andy

Bomb found inside man!

WOUNDED soldier Mario Oliveira left goggle-eyed docs shell-shocked when they opened his chest . . and found a LIVE bomb!

The 22-year-old trooper didn't know what hit him when he felt a searing pain in his chest during a gun battle

At first, surgeons in South Africa thought his gaping wound had been caused by a lethal dum-dum bullet.

But they stepped back in horror when they saw a rifle grenade resting against the sick squaddie's heart.

Sandbags were rushed to the operating theatre to protect the surgeons as they delicately removed the deadly missile.

Murderous sponge mix proves to be recipe for disaster as . . .

FOODMIXER STRANGLES GRANNY

VICTIM...Gwen and (inset) the Rev Kevin Logan

HORRIFIED granny Gwen Little last night said how she was attacked in her kitchen . . . by a bloodthirsty FOOD MIXER!

The gasping gran's face BALLOONED to four times its normal size as the mad machine tried to STRANGLE her with a nylon scarf.

Gwen, who was making a sponge mix for tea, collapsed CHOKING, after the MANIC MIXER sprang into action.

Now speculation is growing that the barmy blender was POSSESSED!

"I was absolutely terrified. I thought I was going to die," said Gwen, 57, as she recovered at her home in Chelmsford, Essex.

"It was like it had a mind of its own. I was preparing a sponge when suddenly my scarf became tangled in the mixer — and I was being strangled."

Eyes bulging, the mother-of-four wrenched the mixer plug from its socket. She stumbled into the garden carrying the machine . . . and was SAVED by a passer-by.

Last night top churchman the Rev Kevin Logan confirmed EVIL SPIRITS were capable of taking over humble household appliances.

"It is the most common type of disturbance exorcists and people in the deliverance ministry come across. It's often called POLTERGEIST activity," he said.

"In our experience in the ministry, it can be caused by evil spirits within the home," said the Church of England vicar from Blackburn, Lancs.

Mr Logan, author of Paganism And The Occult, said he had conducted such services in the form of prayer or communion. More often than not, they were successful.

But at her home, Gwen was vowing not to touch a food mixer again.

By JOHN GARVEY and SIMON FINLAY

She said: "My first instinct was to pull the plug from the wall. Then I collapsed.

"I blacked out then I came round and realised I wasn't able to free myself.

"I had to get to the front door. So I lifted up the machine and carried it. I stumbled to the garden path".

A driving instructor WRENCHED the scarf from Gwen's neck . . . and rushed her to hospital.

Fishy tale on the phone

A frantic man called the cops for help... because he was trapped in a phone booth with a GOLDFISH!

The call box captive was on his way home from a funfair when a gang of thugs struck and tied a rope around the booth.

He told cops: "I've got a goldfish in a bowl and it's going to DIE unless I get out soon.

"People I've not seen before have trapped me in a phone box and put a rope around it."

The unnamed man was last seen heading home to put the fish into a larger bowl after being rescued from his "prison" at Cullompton, Devon by local bobby, PC Harry Bonner.

Cops first thought it was a fishy hoax call and were dealing with a SLIPPERY customer.

---

10 deadly giveaways

HERE'S how you can tell if your household appliances are ALIVE!

1 YOU put your dirty underclothes in the washing machine and it spits them straight back out at you.

2 YOU have to wake your Teasmade up in the morning.

3 YOU have the wife's jaws wired shut and STILL get massive phone bills.

4 THE telly explodes when it's time for Terry Wogan's show.

5 YOU mix the drinks for a party and later the cocktail shaker can't walk in a straight line.

6 YOU arrive home after ten pints of lager and a vindaloo and are almost knocked down by the toilet as it bolts for the door.

7 THE kettle doesn't whistle — it tells you how depressed it's been lately.

8 YOU'RE always hungry in the evenings since the microwave committed suicide.

9 THE bathroom scales say you're putting on weight. They're lying!

10 YOU'RE mixing a cake when the food mixer suddenly grabs your scarf and tries to strangle you!

Hi-rise spook haunts flats

GHOSTBUSTERS have been called to a block of council flats to get rid of the spirit of a DIRTY OLD MAN!

They've been terrorised by footsteps outside their bedrooms and the ghoul's made the Portsmouth flats' electrics go on the blink.

Big lizard-lugs suck-blow shock

THE first land animals on Earth breathed through their EARS, say boffins probing the planet's early life.

A 360 million-year-old lizard discovered in Greenland had breathing rods in its ears says Cambridge University expert Jenny Clack.

ALIEN LOVESLIME KILLED MY PETUNIAS

Lavvy lover

OLD codger Henryk Norkus has amazed his family . . . by locking himself in the bathroom for FOUR YEARS.

Retired welder Henryk, 72, refuses to open the door even though his folks BEG him daily to come out.

Jiffy

"He'd been in there a whole day when I noticed something was wrong. But he kept saying he'd be out in a jiffy, said wife Birgitta, 68.

"He insists it's only constipation and all we can do is wait and hope."

Mental health professionals are now trying to work out what keeps Henryk pinned to his seat.

"All he says is: 'I'll be out in a second' to the psychologists I bring over," sighed his son Ludwig, 39, from his home in Leipzig, East Germany.

EXCLUSIVE

GOBSMACKED builder Chris Till told last night how sex-crazed space aliens covered his garden in killer LOVE-SLIME!

For stunned Chris says a gang of randy ETs wiped out his prize petunias by BONKING in his flowerbeds.

And yesterday top UFO experts confirmed alien nookie-juice left behind after outta-this-world rumpy-pumpy has a DEADLY effect on Earth's plant life.

"I've looked after my garden for years and now these bloody aliens have ruined it," said heartbroken Chris, as he surveyed his yard.

The stunned builder was woken in the middle of the night by groaning noises and spotted two glowing figures HUMPING when he looked out of the window.

Chris, 50, says GALLONS of the slime, which forms an invisible layer over plant life, were left behind.

Covering

And the builder says his son Mick has come out in a MASSIVE RASH after he walked in the garden.

Mick, 27, who also saw the aliens said: "They were about seven feet tall, had extremely large heads, and a green glow from head to foot.

"The next morning I went into the garden and saw loads

BLOOMIN' ANGRY... builder Chris Till

By NICK CRACKNELL

of resinous film covering all the plants and our oak tree.

He said the slime STUCK to his chest causing him to come out in the huge red rash.

"It hurt like hell, but it healed within a couple of days, said Chris.

"This stuff is killing off the garden. I have tried everything known to man to remove it, but nothing works."

Now the desperate family of Petworth, West Sussex, have called in government boffins and begged them to help save the garden.

Top UFO expert Rex Dutter warned Chris and his family to keep away from the garden and branded the slime as DEADLY.

"This slime is obviously the result of the aliens' liaison — it is most unusual, but not unheard of," said Rex, the editor of the influential UFO magazine, Viewpoint Aquarius.

"Aliens have the ability to take on any form they wish.

It is highly probable they took on the form of a copulating earth couple.

"This slime has been seen on various occasions and is known to kill plant life and cause tumours, pimples and rashes to earthlings.

"The slime will disappear in a matter of weeks — but sadly the plants will not grow again."

The Forestry Commission plan to step up their own investigations to beat the slime, David Rose, a Commission spokesman said last night.

IT'S PUSS IN JACK BOOTS

MIXED-up moggie Sam eyes the half — chance of a kill and the opportunity to show his prowess. The power hungry pussy wants to rule the neighbourhood.

MY CAT'S COME HOME AS HITLER

Hans off my puss!

FACTORY-worker Freddie Kendall told last night how his cuddly kitten turned into nasty Nazi Hitler ... and even grew his famous moustache!

And Freddie, 47, reckons his moggie Sam — who's Nazi tash is GENUINE — has even begun to act like the evil Fuhrer.

For sinister Sam has learned the German goose-stepping march and is trying to EXTERMINATE all the felines in the

By SIMON FINLAY

neighbourhood in his crazed struggle for power.

"It's frightening wo watch Sam. He has just changed completely since he was a kitten — now he just wants to invade other cats' territories and drive them off," said Freddie.

"He was such a lovely little kitten. Then he grew his tuft of fur beneath his nose and he's gone bonkers ... he just

wants to be the top cat," he added.

Now bachelor Freddie, of Oregon, USA, is scared that Sam will turn on him.

"It is so hard to tell because he's so unpredictable. One minute he sits purring away, the next he's out scrapping with a tom cat a couple of miles away," said Freddie.

"When he comes back at night he whines and whinges until he gets his food. said Freddie."

Knock, knock

UNLUCKY Millon Hayes was knocked unconscious by a ten-ton truck ... then run over by the ambulance sent to save him on a motorway in Marianna. Florida.

MONSTER...
bug

FRUITY PRAYING MANTIS STOLE MY CHUNKS!

Flo: Soundproofed

Snoring ban on big-noise Flo, 83

PENSIONER Florrie Phillips was branded a noise hazard yesterday ... because of her ear-splitting snores.

Magistrates said her nocturnal grunts and groans broke the Control of Pollution Act.

And they slapped a noise abatement order on 83-year-old Florrie, of Alwoodley, Leeds, who was taken to court by her bog-eyed neighbours.

Sandra Davies, 41, said her 71-year-old husband, Basil, had a bad heart. And the racket from next door had made his condition worse.

Costs

The couple said they made a deal with Florrie to instal £1,500 worth of soundproofing, which had solved the problem.

But they asked the Leeds court for "substantial" costs to cover their legal battle for a good night's sleep.

Their plea was turned down after Florrie's lawyer, Mr Michael Lawrence, said:"Snoring is a natural phenomenon. It's good for the heart and blood pressure."

STUNNED shopper Estelle Tague shuddered with HORROR last night and told how she found a MONSTER Praying Mantis in a pineapple.

Estelle, 19, screamed in terror because she thought the BUG-EYED insect would try to BITE her boyfriend.

He attacked it with a knife—but it clung to the blade. Estelle finally killed it with boiling water and stormed round to Gateway's where she bought the fruit.

Climbed

She said last night: "We got the pineapple from the display and I was about to cut the leaves off at home when my boyfriend said: 'There's an insect in it.'

"It started nipping at his fingers and I SCREAMED because I was afraid it could give a very nasty bite."

Her boyfriend, warehouseman Roger Taylor, 21, said: "I could see this pair of silver eyes. I was sure I knew what it was, panicked and chucked it in the sink.

"But it climbed out, so

ESTELLE...horror

I poked it with a kitchen knife, and it clung to that!"

Finally, trainee accountant Estelle killed it with BOILING water and took it back to Gateway's store near her home in Buxton, Derbyshire, to complain.

Clive Hammond, head of corporate affairs for Gateway's, claimed it was only a STICK INSECT.

He added: "We have no idea where it came from, but we've apologised to the lady."

Pooches pine for Liberace

CAMP pianist Liberace's 23 dogs are still pining for the star more than a year after he died of AIDS.

The heartbroken hounds still haven't forgotten the expensive luxuries — including champagne — lavished on them by their beloved owner.

As the millionaire lay gasping on his death-bed, his only concern was for the pack of pampered pooches.

And he personally asked his housekeeper of 36 years, Gladys Luckie, to treat them like royalty until they too panted their last.

"I often can't sleep at night because of the tortured howls I hear from Liberace's place," said a neighbour near the star's Palm Springs mansion.

"They were never like that before he died. I suppose they really miss him — he loved them like children.

"There are a lot of people crying out for the money Liberace left behind, but at least the dogs are crying for him."

The housewives' heart-throb was convinced he would one day be reunited with the crestfallen canines in heaven.

"I love dogs more than people. Dogs are helpless and they only want love," he said.

Herd about mad Boris

BARMY Boris Gornik was declared dead last night, after a suicide pact — with 46 COWS!

Depressed by mounting debts, the loony yokel THREW himself into a pond . . . and his herd followed.

Frustrated farmer Gornik, 62, of Spisska, Czechoslovakia, was down in the mouth after bailiffs threatened to put down his herd.

ALIENS P**S ON THE SUN

THEY SPOIL THE HEAT WAVE

Top boffin says universe could blow apart if they don't stop

KILLJOY aliens are trying to end Britain's sizzling heatwave . . . by p***ing on the SUN!

And top space watcher Christopher Robinson last night warned that their antics could cool down the sun so much it could EXPLODE and BLOW UP THE UNIVERSE!

The shocking revelations came after renowned astrologer Chris saw FOUR hovering spaceships — one measuring a mind-boggling one MILLION miles long — soaking the sun.

Terrified

"If these aliens carry on they will cool down the sun to such an extend it will expand, causing a situation known as Super Nova," said Chris.

"The sun will get BIGGER and BIGGER and then cause such an almighty explosion the whole world will be blown away.

"I'm terrified. I don't know why they are doing it. Maybe they don't like us.

Spraying

"At first, there was only one medium-sized spaceship spraying jets of waste liquid at the sun — but within days a HUGE craft joined in.

"I have seen numerous space vessels in my time but

EYE EYE . . . Chris spies on aliens

By NICK CRACKNELL

this one was ENORMOUS. A huge jet of water was being sprayed out," he said.

"At first, I thought they didn't like the heat and were doing earth a favour and making it a little cooler for us. But I quickly realised their motive was a lot more SINISTER.

Galaxy

"I fear they want to destroy our galaxy and make themselves the supreme beings."

Chris, 36, of Luton, Beds hit the headlines in 1971 when RAF top brass asked for his help after a spaceship was seen flying over London.

"A high-ranking RAF officer thoroughly de-briefed me. I can't say too much about that situation because it's still top secret," added Chris.

"No doubt my military contacts and I will try to devise a plan to stop these aliens.

"All I can say is that it's going to be TRICKY."

BABY ALIEN ON LOOSE IN BRITAIN!

By GAZZA THOMPSON

THE EVIDENCE: *Alien creature scuttles off for cover in the undergrowth*

THESE are the amazing pictures hailed as PROOF extra-terrestrial life has touched down on British soil.

The incredible snaps — taken by an amateur photographer — were passed to Sunday Sport investigators during a secret meeting in North London.

The pictures clearly show a baby life-form UFO experts say CANNOT be human.

The strange creature has a huge oval-shaped head mounted on a thin bony body.

The snaps were passed to our newsmen after an anonymous telephone caller contacted our London headquarters.

Now the amazing snaps have sparked speculation of a huge Government cover-up to prevent public hysteria.

"It's fascinating. This little guy could be the proof we've all been waiting for,"said top UFOlogist David Barclay.

"Perhaps this is the first evidence they're here," added David, of the respected Independent UFO Network.

The caller who supplied the snaps — believed to be a disgruntled scientist — refused to speak for more than a few seconds on the phone with our reporter.

Nervous

After arranging a secret rendezvous in a deserted car park, the nervous informant said he had a package of "national importance."

Later, he passed a selection of snapshots to our man and claimed they were seized by the authorities. A member of the public with a pocket camera took the snaps.

The shock revelations come just three months after Sunday Sport published a dossier suggesting intergalactic beings visited Earth.

Our evidence included:

FACT: American researcher Stanton Friedman later obtained secret files under freedom of information laws which PROVE authorities launched a cover-up.

FACT: In 1986 an entire town witnessed scores of UFO sightings in broad daylight at Belleville, Wisconsin, USA.

FACT: In October 1989 the official Soviet news agency TASS announced space aliens had touched down and mingled with Russians at Voronezh.

Hugh Pincott of the Association for the Scientific Study of Anomalous Phenomena poured cold water on the authenticity of the photographs.

Believe

"It's hard to believe this actually proves anything," said Hugh.

A furious spokesman for the Ministry of Defence said: "We have never heard of them. We know nothing of them. It is highly unlikely we would have such material," said the spokesman.

THE MEETING: *Rendezvous with boffin* **THE HANDOVER:** *We get pictures*

Questions the nation is asking

WHO took these sensational pictures?

THEY were taken by an amateur photographer using an ordinary, "snapshot"-style camera on colour film. But his identity is surrounded by a cloak of secrecy.

WHY are they so significant?

BECAUSE of the extraordinary amount of detail, and the lack of any apparent trace of trickery — even under the full glare of minute scientific analysis.

WHAT do they show?

EXPERT opinion is divided. Some believe the alien creature, which scientists have calculated is only some two feet tall by comparison with background foliage, is a space CHILD. But others maintain its tiny size is a product of an alien environment.

WHEN were they taken?

FORENSIC tests are believed to have proved beyond doubt that the chemicals used in developing the film are relatively fresh — say, no more than three weeks old.

WHERE were they taken?

PICTURES lack sufficient background detail to pinpoint an exact location. But the background vegetation obviously suggests dense woodland.

IF they are genuine, what are the implications?

ALIENS have landed. But is it a friendly scouting mission . . . or the beginnings of an invasion?

ALIEN: *The photograph that shocked the scientists*

ALIEN SNATCH

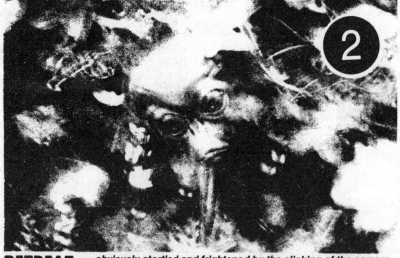

RETREAT ... *obviously startled and frightened by the clicking of the camera, the weirdo alien creature desperately makes a bolt for cover*

ESCAPE ... *an incredible scorching getaway as the thing from outer space scuttles off to its previously undiscovered lair deep in the woods*

FIRST OFFICIAL PHOTOS

By SIMON FINLAY

SHOCKED UFO experts were last night wracking their brains after the discovery of the first-ever pictures of an ALIEN BABY !

The fleeting glimpse of the tiny space creature was captured by an amateur cameraman walking in woodland.

And the sensational photographs are thought to be the proof the world has been waiting for—that aliens are now in Britain.

"There have been numerous claims of sightings in Britain but never pictures," said David Barclay of the Independent UFO network.

The incredible shots were leaked to Sunday Sport by a scientist officially working on projects of national importance.

1 The first shot shows a remarkable close-up study of the alien baby in woodland.

2 The next, after it was alarmed by the camera clicking away, clearly shows the E.T. scurrying into bushes to hide from the photographer.

3 And the final picture in the series sees the matchstick-thin creature dashing out of sight at super-human speed.

■ FULL STORY . . . Page 7

BABY

1

SHOCK *. . . and the strange alien baby is snapped as it emerges from a hiding place in remote woodland undergrowth*

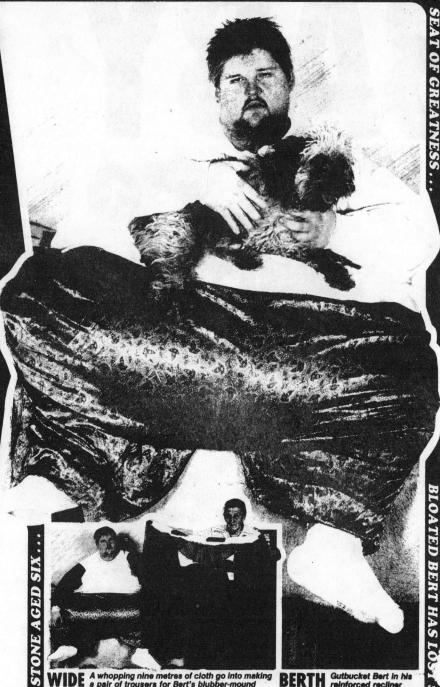

DIETING CAN'T HELP WORLD'S FATTEST MAN SHED POUNDS

SEAT OF GREATNESS...

BLOATED BERT HAS LOST SIGHT OF HIS SHOES...

63 STONE BERT STUCK IN HIS CHAIR FOR 7 YEARS

TWELVE STONE AGED SIX...

WIDE *A whopping nine metres of cloth go into making a pair of trousers for Bert's blubber-mound*

BERTH *Gutbucket Bert in his reinforced recliner*

SIXTY-THREE stone belly-buster Bert Pernitsch told last night how he's so FAT he hasn't left his armchair for ... SEVEN YEARS.

The bloated blubber-mound lives, eats and sleeps in his slob-seat, specially reinforced with huge concrete blocks to hold his weight.

And the last time he left his house, he was hoisted up by builder's CRANE.

Bert, 32, started ballooning when he was only two years old and hit TWELVE STONE on his sixth birthday.

By the time he was 15, he broke his mother's

■ GUTBUCKET Bert only strains himself out of his chair to go to the toilet.

"I really do have problems going," he said.
■ Berts mum Josefine, 65, has to make all of his clothes.

She said: "For trousers I need nine metres of cloth and for shirts, 11 metres."

Man mountain can't sleep lying down or he'll die!

By SIMON FINLAY

scales with his 27 stones of flab.

"I just ate too much and now I can't get rid of the weight," said Bert —whose whopping waistline alone measures nine feet.

"Now I have to sit while I sleep. When I lie on my back, I can't breathe. If I was to sleep on my side, my heart would stop because of the weight," he added.

Doctors even banned him from hospital because he would break

the beds with his porker proportions.

When he was still able to walk, Bert would only go out for a stroll at night because he was afraid someone might LAUGH at him.

He said: "I was afraid of people seeing me. People were chattering, pointing their fingers at me and grumbling.

"I went for walks at night so no one would see me."

"I have tried all sorts of diets. I lose a stone or two and then put it back on again within a week," said Bert of Styria, Austria.

HOSPITAL DOCS BAN BERT FROM A BED...

Who's a REALLY pretty boy then?

HOW TO TELL IF YOUR PET'S A TRANSVESTITE

By DOMINIC KENNEDY

ANIMAL-LOVING Brits were last night issued an astonishing warning from zoologists: "Watch out — your pet could be a POOFDA!"

Bent bunnies, homosexual hounds and camp cats are coming out of the closet all over the land.

Even Britain's forests and fields are being invaded by hordes of kinky cattle and queer deer.

Boffins fear owners who dress male pet's in girlie outfits could even turn them into TRANSVESTITES.

"Young animals such as kittens mount each other experimentally all the time — male on male as well as on female," said animal behaviour expert Roger Mugford.

"If they get the right response from a member of the same sex, they can learn to repeat the behaviour in adult life."

Roger reckons bunnies are the worst species for gender-bending.

"Male rabbits have such an aggressive sex drive they've even been known to mount male CATS," he said.

"The poor cat doesn't know where to look.

"In fact, bizarre sexual behaviour is not unusual in many species of animals.

Booties

"Stallions have been known to mount men, dogs will try to have sex with an outstretched human leg and bulls sometimes take a fancy to the machines which collect their semen."

Now British animals are getting confused about their sex roles as owners force them to wear CLOTHES — like pets in foreign countries.

"It's unnatural for animals to wear bras and panties," said Roger.

Animal psychologist Peter Neville revealed that in France, dogs are made to wear booties, frilly outfits, jogging suits and coats.

"Monkeys wear complete suits of human clothes, dressed and even nail varnish," he said.

"In America, where it's a moral issue, pets are forced to wear knickerbockers so people can't see their genitals.

But not all dogs and cattle who mount members of the same sex are gay, stressed Peter, whose book Do Cats Need Shrinks? is published by Sidgwick and Jackson next month.

FABULOUS FURRY FREAKS . . .

SQUEAK UP . . .

A WUFF DEAL . . .

PONCEY *the parrot, exploiter of feathered freaks or victim of parrot paranoia? Experts are still investigating . . .*

Nine out of ten pooches who expressed a preference said:

Doggy fashion is in!

ANIMAL CRACKE

10 WAYS TO SPOT ANY MONKEY BUSINESS

1. THE tortoise has painted toenails.
2. YOU keep finding yer wig in the dog basket.
3. THE budgie uses its mirror to put on lipstick.
4. THE hamster watches The Clothes Show.
5. YER gerbil's gone and shaved its legs.
6. THE pony wears horse shoes with high heels.
7. THE hen answers to the name of Divine.
8. YOU'VE to unclip the cow's braces for milking.
9. THE goldfish turn yer nets into stockings.
10. THE pigs start wearing mud packs.

FULL MOON special!

MY LIFE OF HELL WITH WEREWOLF RAPIST

FIEND *Jose Rodrigues, the werewolf rapist, who mainly carried out his terrifying crimes when the moon was full...*

HEARTBROKEN wife and mother Wendy Rodrigues last night CHOKED back TEARS as she told how her handsome DREAM hubby turned into a depraved WEREWOLF sex MONSTER.

For the man who married the pretty blonde in a white wedding ceremony, and then fathered their beautiful daughter, RAPED old GRANNIES.

Sicko Jose Rodrigues—banged up this week for 17 years—was dubbed the WEREWOLF rapist because he attacked his victims around the time of FULL MOON.

By day, the loving husband worked hard in a warehouse —and was a DEVOTED dad to 14-month-old daughter Charlotte.

But, by night, he waited for wife Wendy to fall asleep before slipping out to commit monstrous acts of DEPRAVITY against helpless women.

During a three-year reign of TERROR he raped SEVEN times, performed unnatural acts twice and stole his victims' possessions.

■ WEREWOLF rapist Rodrigues stalked the coastal retirement towns of Worthing, Brighton and Eastbourne hunting frail, elderly victims.

■ Often wearing a terrorist-style balaclava mask the sex beast broke into granny-flats and old folks' homes to RAPE and ROB.

■ The Jekyll and Hyde warehouseman's reign of terror ended in February when he was trapped by a brilliant piece of detective work.

■ This week, monster Rodrigues was jailed after admitting seven charges of RAPE, two of BUGGERY and a string of SEXUAL assaults.

One of his victims tried to commit SUICIDE, another suffered memory loss and almost went MAD.

But Wendy only became aware of Jose's NAUSEATING nighttime activities after his arrest.

Distraught

"He seemed so normal—but he must have been schizophrenic," said distraught Wendy, whose world fell apart when she learned the awful truth.

"To me, he appeared a caring husband and a good father to our daughter—but I never felt totally sure about him.

"He was a deep person.

"When he stayed out until the early hours, he always told me he had been working.

"I wasn't quite sure, but I didn't think anything TERRIBLE was happening," she added.

Fearing her husband was sneaking off to see another woman, Wendy kept a DIARY of her LONELY NIGHTS.

Court case special
By RAY LEVINE

settled down to married life did Wendy suspect something might be WRONG.

"We had a lovely wedding ceremony and reception," said Wendy, at the home they shared in Bexhill-on-Sea.

A police investigation involving 65 officers and costing £250,000 was launched to nail granny-grabber Rodrigues.

Starry-eyed Wendy was bowled over by Portuguese-born Jose's swarthy good looks and snappy appearance when they met at the Tropicana disco in Crawley, Sussex.

He was charming throughout their year-long engagement and they wed at Tunbridge Wells in 1983.

It was only as they

POLITE, FRIENDLY AND GOOD FATHER...

SNARED *'polite' monster marries Wendy*

> *I kept a diary of times he left house because I thought he might be seeing another woman*

tion evil Rodrigues was seeking.

The twisted 31-year-old FIEND drove the family's yellow Ford Fiesta to south coast towns. He knew many elderly people lived there.

He gained entry to his frail victims' homes by climbing through windows before launching into his FRENZIED assaults.

A few months later he attacked a 78 year-old arthritic woman and stole her £400 savings.

In April, 1988, an 81-year-old woman woke to find Rodrigues lying on top of her. He demanded

cash then RAPED her TWICE.

As police stepped up their hunt, the attacks became more frequent and VIOLENT.

To stop a 77-year-old woman screaming, Rodrigues pushed her DENTURES down her THROAT.

Slashed

He SLASHED another victim's tights off with a razor sharp KNIFE.

Neither Wendy nor Rodrigues' workmates had any idea the shy immigrant was the WEREWOLF rapist.

Colleague Leslie Gill said "Before his arrest, I had absolutely no suspicions about him.

"Nobody thought there was anything STRANGE about him.

"He had a very good record during the four and a half years he was with us.

"We were all SHOCKED, DISGUSTED and absolutely SURPRISED he was the rapist."

Mr. Gill added: "Up to this time, if I had seen anybody walking along the street I would have been able to tell immediately there was something funny about them.

"But it doesn't happen like that in real life," he added.

Then, in December, 1988, Rodrigues struck at a nursing home for pensioners aged between 80-100—but this time he picked on a 29-year-old care worker.

She grimly told Rodrigues: "I would rather you KILL ME than rape me."

He snarled the ultimatum: "I will give you the choice. I will count to ten."

Eventually, he knocked her about—and indecently assaulted her.

Rodrigues came close to being caught several times. He once gave pursuing cops in a panda car the slip while on foot.

He was finally

cornered by a clever police trap, after a nurse recognised his picture among criminals' mugshots.

When offered a piece of chocolate by Det. Con. Andrew Franklyn, Rodrigues said: "I don't like it. I don't eat it."

The refusal was EXACTLY the same as one he had given a pensioner who tried to BEFRIEND him during an attack.

Sealed

Records revealed Rodrigues rarely showed up for work on the days ater his attacks.

And the secret diary kept by Wendy—who recorded Rodrigues' nights away from home —finally sealed his fate.

"She told us the marriage was BREAKING UP. Rodrigues frequently gave her excuses she didn't believe," barrister Richard Brown told Lewes Crown Court, Sussex.

BUT AT NIGHT HE TURNED INTO A CRAZED BEAST...

Full moon MANIAC Rodrigues' sickening attacks began in November, 1987, when he struck at an 81 year-old widow's warden assisted flat in Crowborough, Sussex.

WIFE *Wendy, who kept a record of when Rodrigues slipped out*

■ PENSIONER Gwenda X, aged 79, told how she came face-to-face with evil Rodrigues.

She said: "I woke and he was lying on top of me on the bed as if he was going to rape me. He put his hand over my mouth so I couldn't scream. I was so frightened.

■ "He didn't speak and he made no attempt to hide his face," she added.

■ As crazed Rodrigues fumbled with the bedclothes Gwenda, whose flat is fitted with a panic button, managed to raise the alarm— and the sex beast fled into the night.

■ "I was so relieved when I heard he'd been caught," added Gwenda.

Monster pigeon pinches pussies

A GIANT pigeon has been nabbing moggies from the balconies of high-rise flats in Barcelona, Spain. The enormous black bird has twice been spotted pinching pussies.

Stolen car left cops clueless!

POLICE were told a stolen car had been dumped at Luton Airport but the make or number weren't known. There are about 15,000 cars parked there every day, says a police mag.

Pool fool lifeguard fished out of water

A RED-FACED lifeguard had to be RESCUED by holidaymakers when he fell into the swimming pool he was supposed to be minding at a holiday camp in Wyke Regis, Dorset.

Museum alert for p*ssed-'ol thief

A THIEF who sparked off a security alert by stealing two pistols from a museum in Weymouth, Dorset, returned there with a note saying: 'Sorry—I was drunk.'

HEATWAVE VICTIM FREEZES HIS

It's a ball bustin' nutty exclusive!

B✶✶✶✶✶KS OFF!

Salesman's frostbite fears after snowballs shocker...

By ANDY 'Cool Hand' HARRIS

POTTY potter Anthony Jones was nursing his frostbitten B*****KS yesterday ...after trying to beat the heatwave by plopping his plums in an ICE BUCKET!

The melting mud-moulder suffered a severe attack of COLD COBBLERS when he attempted to survive soaring temperatures by CHILLING his CHOPPER.

● ANTHONY

Now doctors have warned slapping yer scrotum in ice can lead to DISASTER.

"I was literally sweating my balls off in the office and no amount of cold drinks or choc ices helped," said Anthony, 19, of Stoke-on-Trent.

Crushed

"I got so desperate, an ice bucket seemed the only cure. So I got one from the local, popped into the bog – and dipped my GOOLIES in.

"At first, the relief was FANTASTIC...staggering. I went DIZZY and my whole body cooled."

But, within a few minutes, the hasty hot-head suddenly noticed his nuts SHRIVELLING and turning BLUE!

"As I crouched over the bucket a terrible, searing PAIN shot through my body as if someone had CRUSHED my NUTS between two planks of wood," he said.

"I saw my pride and joy SHRINKING and turning a horrible purply-blue colour.

"I pulled them out pronto. They were virtually DISAPPEARING," he said.

Nursing his painful pride and severely sore scrote, red-faced Anthony tried to see the funny side of his brainstorm.

"It's not the sort of thing I'd do again. But, at the time, it was the only thing I could think of," he croaked.

"But I won't be wearing any TIGHT trousers for a while!"

6 ways to keep yer cobs cool

1. Wear baggy boxer shorts to let the air circulate.....................
2. Shove some cold custard down yer pants..........................
3. Book an air ticket to Alaska.....................
4. Line yer underwear with tin foil early in the morning..............
5. Make love in a vat of ice cream.............
6. Dangle 'em in a thermos flask full of cold water.................

TROTTIN' STAR'S MAD PIG DISEASE

SOW...happy Vic

Crazy comic tells of porky peril!

MADCAP telly comic Vic Reeves last night told how he escaped being mobbed by forty MAD PIGS in a stinking mudbath of CR*P!

The star of Vic Reeves' Big Night Out was TERRIFIED when he got stuck as he fled the snorting porkers.

"I was frightened because I didn't think I'd get away.

"They might have MOBBED ME," said Vic, 31.

Rattling

The Darlington-born funnyman, real name Jim Moir — who's pulling in mammoth audiences for his Friday night Channel 4 show — was chased down a hill by the HUNGRY HOGS.

"I'd gone to feed them and, after leaving their meal out, they could hear the pellets rattling around in the bag and they started coming after me," said Vic.

*"I started running towards the gate but got caught in the foul-smelling mud and cr*p,"* said Vic.

"I had all these crazy pigs grunting and snort-

By SIMON FINLAY

ing around me," added the star.

Vic, once a pig farmer before making the big-time as an entertainer, said: "It was a good life. I might go back to it some day."

He got his first big TV break on The Tube and, later, with Jonathan Ross.

The first Vic Reeves series has been so successful, he's signed up to do a Christmas Special and a sitcom involving Vic and a showbiz pal is also in the pipeline.

Vic, who often pulls stunts on stage, remembered one especially.

"I did this gag with an oven I intended to blow up. I put a load of gunpowder inside and went to light it. It EXPLODED around my hand," he said.

HERE'S ten odd jobs stars did before they were famous!

Craig McLachlin (Neighbours): plumber
Bob Hoskins (Movie Star): trainee accountant.
Michelle Collins (EastEnders): McDonald's girl.
Les Dawson (Comedian): plumber.
Rod Stewart (Singer): grave digger.
Annie Lennox (Singer): fish factory packer.
Paul Hogan (Crocodile Dundee): painter.
Charles Lawson (Coronation Street): gardener.
Jim Davidson (Comedian): butcher.
Pete Dean (EastEnders): barrowboy.

Chocolate willy case stands up

EDIBLE willies have cost the owners of a trendy London shop a £300 fine — after magistrates branded novelties offensive.

The shop — Knutz, in Covent Garden — also had mouth-waterin' items confiscated by Bow Street Court.

An elderly woman had complained to police after seeing a six-year-old boy in the shop.

Sex mad salad science probe

CABBAGE-brained bureaucrats are forking out thousands of American taxpayers' dollars to find out how radishes BONK!

The US government-backed National Science Foundation is spending an incredible $174,000 to discover why wild radishes accept pollen from some radishes and not others.

SPENDING A PENNY NOW COSTS 20P...

BOGSMACKED

Super lav leaves old f*rts hangin' out

By BERTIE OLLOCKS

SOPHISTICATED superloos are making doddery pensioners' lives a misery — by suddenly springing open while they're having a DUMP!

Shocked shoppers in Epping Forest dread getting an eyeful of crumbly having a PLOP in the high street.

And the weeping wrinklies feel so humiliated that some never recover from the TRAUMA.

Now they've launched a campaign for hassle-free cr*ps so they can lay their LOGS to rest at LEISURE.

One elderly victim, who begged not to be named, sobbed last night: "I had to go to the loo while shopping. It takes me rather a long time these days.

"I was barely half-way through when the door BURST OPEN and there I was, in a crowded shopping precinct. I'll never forget the look on people's faces.

The luxury loos, which clean themselves and play soothing music, have a built-in 15 minute time limit after which punters are exposed to the public.

But now oldies are fighting back and Epping Forest District Council in Essex is backing their campaign.

Proud

Councillor Michael Bell said last night: "I have heard concern that the time span is not long enough for elderly to adjust their clothes.

When the music stops, all is revealed."

And a spokesman for Age Concern said yesterday: "It is embarrassing for old people when this happens.

"*They are often proud, and this is very humiliating. We would welcome extra mintues being added to the time.*"

A spokesman for superloo makers, Fleet Equipment of London said: "The time limit is to stop tramps sleeping in the units but there's no reason why we can't extend it if requested.

10 TOP TUNES TO CROON IN THE LOO

1 Superloo Sunset
2 Love You Be-carzey
3 Loo Suede Shoes
4 Pees Pees Me
5 Shake, Rattle 'n' Bog Roll
6 Loo-ey In The Sky With Diamonds
7 All You Need Is Lav
8 The Look Of Loo-ve
9 I Lav, You Lav
10 Loo-ve Is a Many Splendoured Thing

LOO Door blimey! One panicking pooer feels the wind as the superloo suddenly swings open

ROLL Caught cr*pping — but he's barely had time to f*rt

SPACE AGE CONVENIENCES PROVE INCONVENIENT FOR THOSE WHO CAN'T DUMP AND DASH...

BROKEN-HEARTED OLD FOLK SAY DOORS OPEN BEFORE THEY'VE F*RTED

LEISURELY LOG-LAYERS FLUSHED WITH FAILURE

SALESMAN'S AMAZING PSYCHIC LOVE PLUMS

...clever Trevor's alarming eggbag saves his Mummy

By BERTIE OLLOCKS

PSYCHIC salesman Trevor Hammond whipped out his wedding tackle last night and sensationally revealed: "My LOVE PLUMS can predict the FUTURE."

The shy bachelor strokes his gonads until he's in a trance—then stuns punters by telling 'em their destiny.

Trevor, 26, claimed Tarot cards, palmistry and tea-leaves are just crystal BALLS.

Trevor, of North Camp, Hants, claimed he foresaw the Clapham Junction rail disaster and Armenian earthquake during a scrote-strokin' session.

He revealed: "I was quite young when I first discovered my ability.

"I was having a bath and washing my plums when my Mum came in. I told her to drive carefully because I suddenly had this vision of her crashing the car."

Visions

The next day, said Trevor, his sixth sense proved right. His mother was unhurt, but he said: "It began to happen more and more often.

"This strange urge to stick my hand down my Y-fronts would come over me, even in public. Then the visions would come."

Respected psychic David Bingham last night BACKED Trevor's amazing claim.

In a testicle testimonial the eminent chairman of Britain's Astrological and Psychic Society said: "A clairvoyant can pick up vibrations from all sorts of things."

Tycoon gives his missus the bird...

TYCOON Oscar Wenner is divorcing his bird-brained missus, Greta ... after she SUCKED UP his prize budgie in a VACUUM CLEANER!

Accident-prone Greta was cleaning the living room when Diego flew off his perch and was chewed up by the Hoover.

"The suction stopped for a second and I saw something squirming up the hose," said the 42-year-old housewife.

Rage

When he got home Oscar, 46, flew into a rage and filed a lawsuit to end their 12-year marriage.

He had shelled out £6,500 to jet Diego from South America to their home in Essen, Germany.

"I overlooked a lot—but I can't overlook Diego's death," said Oscar.

SECRETS...Friedman

Dossier of shame on aliens

TOP UFO boffins last night revealed they've compiled a sensational dossier proving White House officials tried to cover-up a series of alien sightings.

The amazing revelations came as Sunday Sport prepared to hatch its own alien from an E.T. egg obtained by our newsmen.

Space boffin Stanton Friedman claims to have uncovered a "cosmic Watergate scandal."

"I know the US government and others have covered up information," he said.

Mr Friedman says he has "Top Secret" files that allegedly come from the White House and describe a stunning alien landing on Earth in 1947 when four little BLUE men were killed.

Tiny beings were found dead after crashing their flying saucer near Roswell, New Mexico.

● Sunday Sport newsmen smuggled OUR egg out of Russia after the official news agency Tass reported a UFO landing in Voronezh.

It is expected to hatch an alien in two weeks.

OAP-EN UP!

PENSIONER Maria Raia went to docs with a bad tum — and they found a pair surgical forceps in her gut left there by a Turin doc 15 years earlier.

Clean my cage you stupid bitch!

ABUSIVE PARROT FORCES GRANNY TO KILL HERSELF

PRETTY *to look at, but evil to hear . . . the feathered, foul-mouthed killer bird*

POLLY *drove Nellie Smith mad*

By SIMON FINLAY

HORRIFIED neighbours told last night how tragic granny Nellie Smith took her own life... after being driven to despair by a nagging PARROT.

The softly-spoken 58-year-old Liverpudlian hanged herself with a length of electrical lead after her foul-mouthed pet bird Joey turned her life into a NIGHTMARE.

Neighbours discovered a crumpled suicide note in which Nellie told how the feathered fiend reduced her to tears with cruel taunts about her weight.

The beastly bird's pieces-of-hate campaign included:
- **BRANDING** Nellie a "fat cow" and a "slapper."
- **SHOWERING** the shy grandmother with a torrent of four-letter abuse and constantly demanding bird seed.
- **PECKING** huge holes in Nellie's favourite dress, and.
- **RUINING** a dinner party by chirping "Nellie drops her knickers" in front of guests.

Friends say charge nurse Nellie doted on the sicko parrot when she bought it from a Liverpool pet shop two years ago.

Within months evil Joey was TERRORIS- ING his kindly keeper.

"Nellie loved that bird

PEGS OUT *Nell's note*

like a child and just couldn't take it when Joey started insulting her," revealed neighbour Paul Warren.

"Nellie was convinced Joey got his foul language from watching telly but it was probably one of her four grandsons teaching the bird all the obscenities.

On another occasion widow Nellie listened in disbelief as Joey made crude jibes about her love-life at a party.

The evil parrot chanted 'Nellie drops her knickers' and 'Nellie's had the dustman' in front of guests.

Wreck

A torn suicide note revealed the sad truth about her death. It read: "Joey's turned me into a nervous wreck, I can't take it anymore. Yesterday he called me ugly. I love animals — I'm so sorry."

Animal psychologist Dr Harvey Hardcourt told Sunday Sport: "Pets have personalities. They can be bad as well as good."

Joey was put to sleep by vets.

Woman's 'marriage ordered by aliens'

NUTTY housewife Vicki Williams has told how she was ordered to marry her hubby ... by ALIENS!

Pretty Vicki, 47, claims "voices from another planet" told her to get hitched.

The dark-haired ex-secretary stunned cops by telling them she was visited by men from Mars who took control of her mind.

"They told me to travel Europe on a mission to save the world," she said.

She came out with her amazing close encounter statements, after being arrested in connection with the murder of her 48-year-old husband, Brian, at their home in Hanwell, West London, in January.

Stabbed

He was stabbed to death at the couple's home and his body lay in an upstairs room for four days before police and social workers found it.

Crackpot Vicky suffers from severe schizophrenia, an Old Bailey jury heard.

The jury decided that she was unfit to plead to the murder charge and Judge Richard Lowry sent her to a mental hospital.

TITANIC HAUNTS SAILOR'S WATERBED

JAMES heard eerie voices crying in his mattress at dead of night

Sunken ship's ghostly crew keep 'im awake

A TERRIFIED former Merchant Navy sailor last night claimed victims of the Titanic disaster torment him each night . . . by HAUNTING his WATER BED!

Trembling visibly and clutching a wooden crucifix to his chest, James Dickson, 49, told of eerie voices gurgling in the mattress crying: "I'm DROWNING!"

He has spoken out for the first time since the spine-chilling phenomena began—the day a French diving team desecrated the mass grave by plundering the wreck for treasure.

James, who is related to a lookout who died aboard the liner, sobbed quietly as he said: "These past three years have been hell.

"It sounds so crazy I couldn't bring myself to talk about it. Who would believe a BED could be haunted?"

Chilling

But every night sleepless James hears muffled screams in the bed amid the strains of the hymn "Nearer My God To Thee"—the tune the liner's band played as it took on water.

Above the dreadful din the chilling shout 'It's every man for himself,' can be heard. Those were the words yelled in mortal fear by the Titanic' captain as the unthinkable happened and the "unsinkable" sank.

And the noises start at 11.40 p.m. each night—the time the iceberg tore into the hull of the floating palace.

Divorced James, of Portsmouth, Hants, confessed he bought the water bed to cheer himself up when his wife left him in 1970.

He said: "I was suddenly off the leash and wanted to prove I could still be popular with the ladies.

He was already in the Merchant Navy when, in his 20s, a cousin told him a great uncle had perished as a crewman aboard the ill-fated liner which sank off Newfoundland on its maiden voyage in 1912 with the loss of 1,513 lives.

Said James: "It didn't mean much to me. I left the Navy when I was 32 and became a salesman."

So it was an incredible shock when the noises began in 1987. At the time, a French diving crew was being branded a bunch of "pirates" for looting the wreck.

James said: "I thought I was imagining it. I decided to get rid of the bed—but I can't. It's something I can't explain. All I can do is pray for those lost souls."

Leading psychic researcher Paul Eyles said last night: "These poor souls are re-living their last moments through Mr. Dickson who, although he may not know it, is obviously a clairvoyant."

By BERTIE OLLOCKS

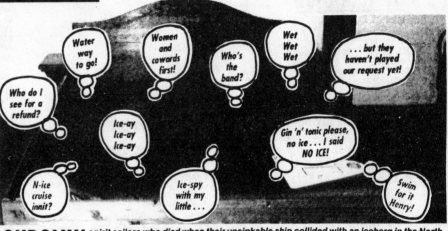

GURGLIN' spirit sailors who died when their unsinkable ship collided with an iceberg in the North Atlantic nearly 80 years ago have found a final resting place in a water . . . bed

HAUNTED BEDPAN CREATES A STINK...

By BERTIE "Odd Job" OLLOCKS

WINDFALL *But unlucky Bob's not doing the business*

ANTIQUES dealer Bob Harvey was facing shutting up shop last night — because of a haunted BEDPAN.

The tormented trader's customers are deserting in droves since he bought the thing — 'coz the 19th century pisspot is POSSESSED!

Several times a week, he comes down from his flat above his tiny shop in Alresford, Hampshire, to open up . . . and finds a farting phantom has taken a sly crap in the old pottery convenience.

Bewildered Bob, 70, said: "I hear terrible noises like someone breaking wind in the night, but I'm too scared to go down to look."

Bob bought the pot at a trade fair eight months ago and things began to go wrong as soon as he got it home. There were strange noises and smells around the home.

Punters stared accusingly at him whenever there was a pong and began avoiding his shop.

Suspicious

Said Bob: "It's terribly embarrassing. Even my wife Audrey gives me funny looks when we come down in the morning and there's a mess in the pan.

"I keep telling her it's haunted . . . but I'm not sure she believes me because a few weeks ago I had a drink with the lads and took a pee in the garden."

"Because I bought it from an antiques fair instead of a shop, I have no way of tracing its former owner.

"Now I'm right in it!"

WATER SENTENCE!

DECORATOR Grant Cumberpatch, of Southwark, London, was jailed for six years after holding up a post office with a water pistol!

Moggy lovin' housewife's horror attack by talkative killer dolly

EXPERTS in the supernatural have been baffled by reports of an invasion . . . of KILLER RAGDOLLS.

Author Lyall Watson makes the amazing revelations in his new book The Nature of Things.

One terrified US housewife has told of the night she nearly croaked — after being throttled by her doll.

"She discovered it in her bedroom holding a button which had been yanked off her nightgown," said Watson, whose book went on sale in Britain this week.

Jinxed

And in Melbourne, Australia, eight-year-old Nicole Hart told Watson: "I talk to my doll all the time, but she never talked back to me before.

"I though it was really neat until she started talking about my cat Jinx. She said Jinx was going to die."

Jinx was run over and killed by a car later that day.

Now psychic researchers are calling on local authorities to set up dumps where worried parents can dispose of danger dolls.

Bingo Fred's winning line

BINGO! Brainy caller Fred Harrington's got such a winning line they've given him a degree.

The Weymouth wonder was awarded a BSc in Applied Bingology after impressing a Yankee visitor.

Game crazy Joan Johannes recommended Fred—he's clickety-click (that's 66) years old—after seeing him in action.

The certificate, awarded by dotty dons at Pasadena University's Faculty of International Bingo, in California, now hangs in his home . . . next to dozens of teddy bears and lampshades won through the game.

Saucy streaker gives grans rise

COPS arrested a man who streaked through the grounds of an old folks home in Siegen, West Gerany, every morning. But he was released after grans said he had brightened up their day.

SEX-MAD SATANIST STUFFED GIRL INTO SUNDAY ROAST

BAKED...Cheryl

EXCLUSIVE

HOUSEWIFE Cheryl Horton last night relived the moment Satanists STUFFED her in a baking box and turned her into Sunday ROAST.

In the week a frightening NSPCC report rocked Britain with revelations of Satanic MURDER, ex-cult sex-slave Cheryl confessed to:

● EATING her own chopped up babies.
● BEING forced into SEX orgies.

■ FULL STORY — PAGES 10-11

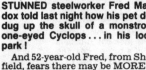

■ YER down-to-earth Sunday Sport ALWAYS guarantees to dig up the BIG stories. So when Fred Maddox (left) made his gruesome find we sent investigator SIMON FINLAY (above) to Grave's Park to unearth the grisly facts . . .

CYCLOPS SKULL FOUND IN SHEFFIELD

STUNNED steelworker Fred Maddox told last night how his pet dog dug up the skull of a monstrous one-eyed Cyclops . . . in his local park !

And 52-year-old Fred, from Sheffield, fears there may be MORE of the terrifying creatures buried under the playing fields.

■ CYCLOPS is the terrifying one-eyed beast of Greek mythology, a giant cave dweller and shepherd. Story-teller Homer says Odysseus got him drunk, stabbed him in the eye with a heated stake-point and stole his sheep while escaping his clutches.

"There could be a whole army of the things lying under there for all I know. It's all so scary," said frightened Fred.

Boffins were stunned when they heard of Fred's freak find, be-

EYE-POPPIN' EXCLUSIVE

lieved to be the remains of a creature thought to be a myth until now.

Scientists urged him to have the gruesome, white bonce-bone examined immediately to discover how long the bug-eyed beast has been under British soil.

Fred confessed he was mystified when he saw

his Cocker Spaniel digging away on a small patch of open ground in GRAVE'S PARK, Sheffield.

"He must have dug down about two feet when he started barking really excitedly. Then he pulled out this round thing about the size of a football."

It was then that Fred

realised it was a SKULL —with only ONE eye socket.

"Even as a skull, it looked like a Cyclops. It was horrible," he added.

Dr. Richard Morris, of the Council of British Archeologists, was shocked when he heard of the find.

"I've never heard of such a thing myself, but I can't say that mutations don't exist," said Dr. Morris, a Research Officer for the CBA.

"I have come across many skeletons and skulls in my work but never one with only one eye."

CABBIE GOES BACK TO THE FUTURE

TIME-TRAVEL EXCLUSIVE

By SIMON FINLAY

TERRIFIED taxi-driver Pete Fay last night told how his cab turned into a TIME-MACHINE...and drove him back 100 years!

Petrified Pete came face-to-face with a grisly ghoul from 1889 which dodged his hurtling mini-cab by walking THROUGH a wall.

And in a horrifying real-life Back To The Future movie drama, the driver was zapped into 1989 again as his car screeched to a halt.

White-faced Pete, 41, shook with fear as he recalled how he nearly bumped into a stable-hand from the Victorian era.

"I have never been so scared in all my life," confessed the cabbie from Bolton, Lancs.

"He walked through a stone wall 3ft thick. He was dressed in black with a waistcoat, and his breeches were tied just below the knee.

"I braked hard to avoid hitting him — but he'd already been dead for a hundred years.

"It was almost as if my car had turned into a time-machine and I was taken back in time. It was very frightening.

GHOST STORY ... petrified Pete

HE'S BACK ... Fox

The ghostly journey through the time warp happened outside an historic country restaurant which was once a stopping point for stage coaches.

Haunted

And the ancient building is now believed to be haunted by a one-time Lord of the Manor and his servants.

Now father-of-two Pete won't go within a mile of the place in case he slips into another black time-hole.

"I was so terrified by the whole thing the hairs were standing up on the back of my neck," he admitted.

Fellow cabbies found Pete slumped in a chair back at the depot after the trauma.

"He was as white as a sheet when he came back here," said boss Vince Southern.

"I've had to keep him off the road until he gets his nerve back."

ALIEN ALLIES

IF space aliens attack earth, Russia and the United States should join forces to zap them, Ronald Reagan told President Gorbachev at their first summit, it has been revealed.

Jerry on sex roll

SEXPOT Jerry Hall plans to spend her retirement...BONKING a Rolling Stone!

Mick Jagger's model girlfriend has decided to carry on having crinkly crumpet in her twilight years.

Glands

"I hope I'll still be enjoying sex which I'm 90," said blonde beauty Jerry.

"I believe sex is good for your health. Physically, it's good for the hormones and glands and, emotionally, it's good to be wanted."

Jerry, star of Hysteria 2, tonight's Aids benefit on Channel 4, is nick-named Co-Co...because she's got size ten FEET!

Ripper's mum and her mates hack up builder as...

LESBIAN WITCHES PLOT TO BRING BACK HITLER!

THE bizarre episode sent shockwaves the normally peaceful city of Milwaukee, the brewing capital of America.

"We've never had anything like this happen here," said Detective Marks. "It's a very conservative working town.

"The people are stunned to think this weird cult was in their midst."

WITCH... 'Ripper's mum' Deborah Kuzack

SICKENED cops told last night how a gang of lesbian witches plunged an axe into their pal's head in a bizarre bid to bring back HITLER.

The twisted women tried to CHOP-UP and EAT builder Jeff Meka, in a gut-churning black magic ritual designed to raise the Fuhrer from the grave.

Yesterday the three evil hags were behind bars after their victim was found roaming the streets DRENCHED in blood.

"They were going to dismember him, drain all his blood and then devour his kidneys," revealed stunned detective Gary Marks, who said he believed the women were lesbians.

Wicked Deborah Kuzack, 26, told the gobsmacked officer that she was Jack the Ripper's long lost MOTHER, and desperately wanted to be reunited with her son, as well as the Fuhrer.

Her two, blood-crazed bed-buddies Catherine Lipsham, 22, and Ramona Barry, 27, were obsessed with evil and thought that human sacrifice would bring back the dictator.

The three wild women lured labourer Jeff to their flat in Milwaukee, USA, saying they were terrified of a passing thunderstorm and needed company.

But when he arrived they pounced on him and sank a HATCHET into his skull.

Chanting

"He had only been at the flat for about five minutes when he went to the toilet," said detective Marks.

"As he finished urinating he heard something from the shower, and turned round to see two if the women in the bath.

"One of them had an axe and they were chanting 'Redrum' which is murder backwards," he said.

"She swung the axe at him and caught him on the forehead. It came down through his eyebrow and caught his eyelid."

KILL FOR LIFE

BLOOD THIRSTY Catherine Lipsham believed she was Jack the Ripper's mother in another life and if she killed to prove her love, he would come back to life, the court was told.

Hags planned to devour pal in gory ritual

"He bolted from the apartment with blood pouring from his head, and by the grace of God an ambulance was passing and picked him up."

Planned

Jeff, a 26-year-old unemployed brickie, underwent emergency treatment and needed more than 100 stitches in his head.

The detective added: "They told me the whole thing was planned.

"Ramona is obsessed with HITLER — she loved him and wanted to bring him back to life.

"They went through a weird ceremony and claimed to have called up SATAN, but so far they'd failed with Jack and Adolf."

"They had held seances, to try to raise evil spirits.

"The victim doesn't look too bad now, but he'll always have a big scar on his head."

The women are now behind bars in Milwaukee, awaiting trail for attempted murder.

WICKED... witch Ramona Barry

Adolf's secrets

■ EVIL Nazi Nancy-boy Adolf Hitler was the biggest POOFDA in history. Last year, your fun-loving Sunday Sport shocked the world by revealing the kinky Kraut was as BENT as a pink Panzer tank and loved to dress as a WOMAN.

■ Years after his death, pictures of the dotty dictator were discovered — showing him wearing a DRESS!

■ Then, on the 100th anniversary of his birth in April, we revealed that the fruity Fuhrer: FARTED uncontrollably during his frequent temper tantrums; PANTED foul breath into the face of a Hollywood movie queen; SLOBBERED into her mouth as he tried a French kiss; RIPPED her clothes off; and PUMPED her "like a dog."

SCHTUNNA... Adolf in drag

BATMAN MENDS CARS IN BRISTOL

BRUCE WAYNE IS A FAKE

Dark knight's boring days with spanner

By JOHN GARVEY

MECHANIC Kevin Townsend RIPPED off his mask and stunned the underworld last night by sensationally revealing . . . "I am BATMAN!"

For an incredible 15 YEARS, the caped crimebuster FOOLED his workmates with his bizarre double identity.

To them, he is the mild-mannered car mechanic who fixes engines for a living.

But, when darkness falls, wimpy Kev DISAPEARS. In his place is an awesome avenger — the legendary DARK KNIGHT!

For more than a decade, Kevin kept his secret. Even the cops in his home city of Bristol denied his existence.

But when Sunday Sport's newshounds tracked him down — to a CAVE in the Cheddar Gorge — he confessed: "It's true. I'm the bloke you're after."

Kevin, 35, revealed how:
● KERSPLAT! He copped his first robbers, after dressing as a bat for a fancy-dress party.
● KAPOW! He leaped from a rooftop to KO a pair of muggers.
● ZONK! He gave baffled police the slip when they tried to unmask him.

Kevin — his cover blown — has agreed to reveal his amazing, TRAGIC history for the first time.

This is his story . . .

❝ I was always regarded as a bit of a WIMP at school. And, just like Bruce Wayne, I saw violent crime at an early age. I was MUGGED when I was 12.

Then, when I was 20, I went to a party dressed in a Batman costume.

On the way, I saw two men trying to grab a woman's handbag. I don't know what happened, but next thing I LAID INTO them, and they were on the ground. ❞

The experience had a profound effect on Kevin and, for the next 12 months, he LOCKED himself away and began perfecting Kung Fu and developed skills in acrobatics and electronic WIZARDRY.

SLEEPY . . . Batman relaxes at the end of the night and, left, the real Kevin

DIRTY BUMS BOMB BOGS!

By JOHN GARVEY

NE of England's sleepy seaside towns was gripped by fear last night — at the mercy of Britain's first TOILET TERRORISTS.

The bizarre wave of BOG-BOMBING is being waged by crazed fanatics demanding home-rule for Dorset.

Police, MPs and fire chiefs yesterday united to condemn the campaign after the latest kamikhazi outrage.

But as the latest blast blew another loo to bits, BOGSMACKED cops confessed: "They've left us with nothing to go on."

They have vowed to step up patrols near public conveniences as local Tory MP Sir James Spicer stormed: "This is a tragedy of the worst order."

He urged police to FLUSH OUT the barmy bog-bombers and said: "Sooner or later, the police are going to catch up with these people.

"I just hope that, when they do, the magistrates will deal with them very severely."

Sir James added: "Our part of the country is the most beautiful place in the world, and to have this mindless stupidity is almost beyond belief."

Cider-swigging separatists are being blamed for the blazes which rip through the loos.

HIT-AND-RUN ALIENS LEFT ME FOR DEAD

DRIES

Mystery of crash during eclipse

WATCH THIS SPACE FOR MORE GOODIES

OUTTA THIS WORLD EXCLUSIVE!

TERRIFIED motorist Marcus McAdam last night told how his car was turned into a twisted wreck... by a hit-and-run SPACESHIP.

The shell-shocked 18-year-old claims he was left for dead after striking the luminous alien craft on a deserted road during the lunar eclipse.

He blacked out moments before the impact, which CRUSHED his red Austin Metro to a PULP, and woke up two hours later outside a hospital.

"I can't remember the actual crash or how I got to hospital," said Marcus last night.

"I was driving home and I saw an oval-shaped light in the sky which zoomed past my car. I thought it was a plane.

"It seemed to land just over the horizon on the road," claimed Marcus.

Miraculously, he escaped with only cuts and bruises.

And Marcus, of Heath Hill, Milton Keynes, is adamant there were no other cars on the road moments before the smash.

Damaged

"I couldn't have hit a car. It was almost six in the morning and I was the only person on the road," said Marcus, who was returning home after watching the most recent lunar eclipse.

"The breakdown service said the car must have hit a metal object to be so badly damaged — but there was no sign of another car.

"I certainly didn't hit a tree. There was no bark embedded in the paintwork and none of the trees along that stretch of road were damaged," added Marcus a producer for local radio station Chiltern Radio.

Mystery still surrounds what happened between the time of the crash, which happened on the A5, and his arrival at hospital.

He was discovered unconscious in the wreckage by a lorry driver, who rushed him to Milton Keynes General — and left without giving his name.

Last night a top UFO investigator backed up Marcus's amazing claim and revealed hit-and-run aliens

MYSTIFIED... Marcus

have struck BEFORE.

"There have been similar well-documented cases," said David Kelly, of the independent UFO Network.

"The craft usually follows the car and lands some distance ahead."

■ **THEORY ONE:** Marcus hit a cosmic captain's spacecraft. The dark sky during the lunar eclipses signal led a massive increase in UFO sightings.
■ **THEORY TWO:** he hit an Iranian helicopter on a mission to kill Satanic Verses author, Salman Rushdie.
■ **THEORY THREE:** Marcus hit a GIANT ANT which mutated after being exposed to Chernobyl radiation.

KEEP YOUR FEET ON THE GROUND TODAY FOLKS!

ALIENS IN ET BOND

STAR-trekking psychic Ruth Norman last night told how she travelled to 32 planets — and made it back in time for TEA.

The perky pensioner claims she's had dozens of close encounters of the unearthly kind.

Ruth, 89, from California, said: "I am a universal emissary throughout the Milky Way.

"I've brought together other world's leaders to Interplanetary Confederation."

Nuke food glows blue

STUNNED scientists have discovered that irradiated food GLOWS BLUE in the dark.

The treatment is meant to kill naturally occurring bacteria in meat and vegetables.

Scientists, struggling to find a method to detect irradiated food, have discovered that, when heated, it gives off a blue glow when the lights are off.

Missing 50 years...it lands at HEATHROW
WORLD WAR 2 BOMBER BACK FROM MOON

THE World War Two bomber which **stunned military bosses by landing on the moon has secretly touched down at HEATH-ROW.**

Security forces launched a massive cover-up after the plane suddenly showed up on British radar screens earlier this week.

Last night the aviation

world exploded in amazement after Sunday Sport released this image-intensified picture of the bomber on Heathrow's tarmac ... and revealed two of the bomber's pilots are STILL ALIVE!

Confused and unshaven, the pilots were ushered through Heath-

row's Terminal Two by security staff.

But they spoke briefly to our newsmen who have been working on the story for two years.

"Its been one hell of a mission," confided Captain Frank Bing.

"We were supposed to bomb Berlin but suddenly got sidetracked."

FULL STORY-pages 10/11

CAPTURED *Bomber snatched using an image intensifier at Heathrow*

Bunny catch angler's caught on hop

FLABBERGASTED fisherman John Sharrock knew something was out of PLAICE when he hauled a 9lb RABBIT from the Thames this week!

The avid angler landed the hare-brained bunny after a 15-minute fight from his fishing perch at London's Docklands.

"There was a sharp tug on my line and I knew something was taking the bait," said the 22-year-old computer wizard.

Skimming

"Then I saw these two fluffy "fins" pierce the water. It was like a mini JAWS skimming below the surface. Then it began swimming towards the middle of the river.

"That bunny put up one hell of a battle but died soon after being netted.

"My missus didn't believe me when I walked through the door with a dripping rabbit on my rod," he added.

UFO crew mega-tom tip farmer reaps 20 pounders

By ALAN WHEELER

GREEN-FINGERED space aliens showed a farmer how to grow tomatoes as big as PUMPKINS.

Stunned scientists are now probing the mouth-watering monsters, which have grown to a GIGANTIC 20 pounds each.

The grateful farmer says the galactic gardeners, who visited him in a UFO, have saved him from bankruptcy now he can grow bumper crops.

"I was sitting in the field when I spotted a shooting star," said Mario Cordato, describing his out-of-this-world encounter.

Curious

"It came towards me and settled in a nearby grove of trees. I was frightened but curious, so I ran to the craft.

"*I found a large metal sphere about 25ft high. A door opened and three man-like creatures came out.*

"They were no more than five feet tall and wore silver suits. Their skin was very white and they had no hair or ears.

"I don't recall them making any sounds, but it seemed like they were talking in my head," said the stunned landowner of Melo, Uruguay.

The space beings used their advanced alien knowledge to tell Mario exactly the right time to plant, the pattern of ploughing and precise amounts of fertilizer to use.

Scientists are now doing soil tests on Mario's 4-acre farm to see if the aliens sprinkled any magic space dust to boost the size of his veggies.

DAZED AIRMEN...

HUSH-HUSH LANDING OF WAR PLANE ON MOON...

TWO dazed airmen, who piloted a World War Two bomber to the Moon, have stumbled — alive and well — into London's Heathrow Airport arrivals lounge.

Their INCREDIBLE appearance followed an unscheduled emergency landing — and immediately sparked a major security scare.

Stunned British authorities ordered a massive top-level COVER-UP operation, claiming instead that five people were arrested trying to SMUGGLE nuclear triggers to Iraq.

The story was instantly swallowed and splashed across the front pages of Fleet Street's midweek editions.

But, today, we can bring you the TRUTH behind the drama.

The bewildered American pilots, looking frightened and unshaven, were bundled into a car with blacked-out windows, shortly after their arrival on Wednesday night.

Captured

They were later whisked away in an official Government car.

But Sunday Sport newsmen got there FIRST after an anonymous tip-off from an airport official, and snatched a world exclusive interview.

And our man captured the bomber itself — using an image-intensifier — sitting on Heathrow runway next to a British Airways jet.

Initially, the men were only prepared to give their name, rank and serial number.

They blurted out their spine-chilling tale after we convinced them the war was OVER and Hitler was dead.

Amazingly, the airmen believed it was 1944 and insisted they were in their 20s — even though they looked like OLD MEN.

● FIRST to break his silence was Captain Frank Bing, who said he was 25.

He claimed:

❝ We were on a top-secret mission over Central Europe in an area known for its mysterious aerial phenomena. There were five of us altogether.

Some of the guys were joking about the place being jinxed, so we thought it was a joke when the co-pilot called to us there was a strange craft approaching.

We didn't bother to

THEORY ONE

■ SPACE aliens could be trying to change the course of world history by showing off their amazing powers to humans.

It may be part of a greater plot to one day overthrow Earthlings as the rulers of our planet and set up a bizarre ET colony.

The Bomber-on-the-Moon saga is just showing world leaders how powerful they can be.

THEORY TWO

● THE bomber was catapulted to the Moon by a black hole above the Bermuda Triangle. The two crewmen survived because their bodies went into a form of space hibernation known by scientists as suspended animation.

They woke when NASA tried to tow them back in December 1988 — but the rope snapped then had to glide down to Heathrow.

THEORY THREE

EVIL Nazi nancy-boy Adolf Hitler — exposed as being a woman by Sunday Sport — is responsible.

The goose-stepping Fuhrer — believed by many to be living in an oxygen tent on the Moon — used secret Nazi war technology to hijack the bomber.

He planned to escape back to Earth aboard the stolen warplane.

HAPPY *Bing and Pott (right) with the rest of the crew before the fateful mission*

MOON struck Captain Bing and Lt. Pott who flew off on a top-secret mission into the Bermuda Triangle

TERRIFYING FEELING OF FALLING . . FALLING . . IN SPACE

LANDING Sunday Sport photographers used an image intensifier at Heathrow to pick up the Privateer as it stood beside a British Airways jet after its amazing journey into space

look, until we heard shouting coming from the cockpit. They sounded PANICKY and YELLED they were were losing control.

After that, I guess I don't remember anything too well, except for a sensation of falling. I felt dizzy and faint.

Colleague

His colleague, Lt Hymie T Pott, took up the EERIE story. He said:

When we came to, there was just me and Frank — the others were GONE, disappeared. I couldn't move or speak, But I could see through the cockpit window up front that it was black outside.

It wasn't like a natural darkness, as if we were flying at night. It was like PITCH. God knows what happened to the rest of the crew . . .

The pair claimed they set off on their mission aboard the United States Air Force Consolidated Privateer — a maritime bomber plane used during the war — on March 16, 1944.

They said they believed they were the victims of an elaborate hoax, until we showed them a copy of the Sunday Sport dated April 24, 1988.

The front page story, headed: *World War 2 Bomber Found On Moon*, was how the world first learned of the stranger-than-fiction drama.

Initially, Moon-scans showed a plane resembling a B52 but clearer shots revealed it to be a Privateer.

Both men claimed the next thing they remember was waking in the hold of the plane.

They dashed to the cockpit to find it empty, and the plane losing altitude rapidly.

Capt Pott grabbed the controls and tried, unsuccessfully, to make radio contact with the ground.

Unknown to the shell-shocked airmen — desperately trying to control their ancient bomber — they were heading for HEATHROW!

After our amazing interview, the airmen were whisked away to a waiting car and driven off.

We were prevented from following, and when we asked where the men were being taken, we were told: "What airmen?"

Officials and Heathrow later DENIED the incident.

April 1, 1990, will go down as a great day in aviation history.

Suddenly, the aircraft, identified as a wartime marine Privateer, which could be seen plainly on the Moon through our powerful telescope on top of the Sunday Sport's building VANISHED. The mystery deepened until . . .

This was Sunday Sport's amazing world-shattering exclusive which broke the incredible news that an American bomber had been found on the Moon and featured in this newspaper on April 24, 1988. This was amazing enough, but . . .

Our investigators discovered the aircraft had taken off from the Moon and was seen lost in space, drifting helplessly in orbit. Little hope was held out for any airmen still being alive. But two of them were and they did a crazy manoeuvre which tipped the plane's nose down towards Earth . . .

GOVERNMENT OFFICIALS CALL FOR IMMEDIATE COVER-UP

EDITOR'S COMMENT

WE regard today's front page as a Sunday Sport classic. In the years to come, it may be worth a lot of money.

You'd be well advised to keep a copy of today's paper in MINT CONDITION — it might make you rich in your old age.

Lee-zy way of listening to radio

STUNNED housewife Dawn Dueberry was FLUSHED with embarrassment last night, after calling the cops to complain her BOG started TALKING to her!

Calls began flooding in from Dawn's neighbours, about the talking toilets. Dawn, 35, of Los Angeles, was relieved to hear the plumbing was picking up a radio station.

WILLIES HOLD YA BIGGEST SECRETS

By BERTIE OLLOCKS

A MIDDLE-AGED mum has declared she wants to start a study of over ONE THOUSAND men's willies — to dick-scover the secret of their personalities.

Fifty-year-old Betti Simpson-Shaw of Hampstead, London, claims her project would show that more accurate readings of men's characters can be made than using traditional methods.

So she's asking scores of wives and girlfriends to try out their own fellas' plonkers — and send her the results.

And the experts have backed her theory — dubbed 'Phallusology.'

"I talked to some doctors about it and said that if you can make judgements about someone from fingerprints or palms, surely something as unique as the penis will speak the truth," said Betti.

LOOKING . . . Betti

__They said it was entirely possible and now I need to carry out a survey to get the evidence.__

"I will be asking women to inspect their husbands' members and make notes about their personalities and I will study the survey returns to spot underlying trends.

"Every man I have spoken to about it has offered to become the subject for a penis reading session — I got fifteen offers in one day," she said.

__To her surprise the whacky willy study has excited firm interest in the psychic world.__

Leading expert David Bingham, chairman of the British Astrological Psychic Society, is convinced Betti has unwittingly got hold of the hard facts.

"If she is a 'Sensitive' she might be able to peel back anything and everything about the person whose willy is being read," David told Sunday Sport.

Dirty dung death trap gave Huns the hump...

NASTY Nazis were blown to bits by exploding camel DUNG in one of the war's most secret — and smelly — operations.

Jeep-loads of Jerries were sent to meet their maker in a shower of S*** in the North African desert, it was revealed last night.

Boffins based in a manky MACARONI factory turned out the turds of terror to defeat Rommel's Afrika Korps, a new book states.

Written by unsung hero private Chuck Jones, it tells how Desert Rats made Hitler's hordes in the Sahara wish they'd stayed in BEDOUIN.

Manure

"Because of the monotonous landscape in North Africa, soldiers deliberately drove into heaps of manure," ex-private Jones said last night.

So Chuck and other boffins held their noses and packed explosives into the dung.

They also turned out fake coal that blew up when it was shovelled into furnaces, and exploding hammers that slave workers smuggled into factories.

Finally, from their base in Monopoli, Italy, the screwy scientists turned out lightbulbs that blew up when they were switched on.

Details of how the boffins gave the Hun a headache are in the hardcover Trojan Horses, published by The Bodley Head.

Bang bang you're dead

A GUNMAN demanding £150,000 wrapped a package around a bank manager's neck, saying it was explosive. But Paris bomb disposal men found it was a string of sausages

UP THE POLE

POTTY Pole Janusz Chomatek has smashed his world record for heading a tennis ball nonstop bouncing a ball on his bonce 15,225 times in 105 minutes.

GUINEA-PIGS

DOCTORS are using pigs' trotters to practise skin surgery techniques, in courses run by the British Association of Dermatologists.

Evil spirits see red and kill 60

ANGRY ghosts caused a bus crash which killed 60 farmers in Zimbabwe, Africa, because of the vehicles colour, a medium claims. Natives associate the colour red with death.

● MUMMY MAN Corky Raa started working like an ancient Egyptian 14 years ago.

A hundred people have already coughed up £7,700 for him to preserve their bodies in the style of the Pharaohs.

SCENT STAMPEDE

COW SHEDS in the US are smelling more sweetly since scientists at Auburn University discovered perfumed cows yield more milk.

It's all alien to rivals...

LANDING . . . They're here

SHELL-shocked docs rocked the world last night when they detected a faint HEARTBEAT from Sunday Sport's own ALIEN EGG.

Boffins sent a SCRAMBLED message to our HQ from their secret, underground lab to announce: "My God — it's ALIVE."

The coded note was disguised to baffle our so-called rivals as they search for our inter-galactic biologist's bolt-hole.

Our on-the-spot reporter revealed: "The atmosphere is electric.

"It happened a few hours ago when they were doing a routine, ultra-sound scan of the egg."

He added: "They detected movement in the alien foetus

By JOHN GARVEY

last week, but this is a real breakthrough.

"The rib-cage is clearly visible and the alien heartbeat can be discerned."

Sunday Sport sent a team of newshounds to POACH the egg from Red scientists three weeks ago after the official Soviet News Agency, Tass, reported an ET invasion.

"We're footing the bill for a CRACK team of doctors to maintain a 24-hour vigil until the hatching in two weeks' time.

Biological computers predict the infant ET will be covered in SCALES, and have THREE eyes.

SAUSAGE SEX PEST STALKED WPC

Poloney groper gave cops space alien baloney

SAUSAGE-wielding sex pest Alan West claimed he was a space alien when cops nabbed him for groping a pretty special constable's BOTTOM!

Banger barmy West, 45, brandished a small poloney sausage as he fondled a WPC while she leaned over a supermarket checkout.

And the pest, who nicknamed his victim "Miss Pilchard", was jailed this week, after a judge branded him a "total nuisance".

A court heard that, after touching her bottom, wild West asked: "Are you praying for a man?"

Then, brandishing the German sausage at her, he demanded: "Or will this do?"

The victim — an off-duty special constable whose name we have withheld — ordered him out of the store.

"Why?" he asked. "Are we going to have sex?"

Stopped

The woman then followed West as he left the shop, but he stopped suddenly, causing her to bump into him.

West then rubbed himself against her boobs, saying: "You have lovely, firm breasts. I know I could do something for you."

By DOMINIC KENNEDY

The woman told the jury at Dorchester Crown Court: "He remarked I had lovely blue eyes and they were even lovelier when I was angry."

When arrested, West told cops: "I come from another planet. I'm not really here."

Wacky West, of Stanley Place, Bridport — who was Dorset's most UNWANTED man — has been banned from all the county's libraries and Gateway supermarkets, where the attack happened.

Jonathan Fuller, prosecuting, said the case could go down in legal history as "Miss Pilchard and the poloney sausage".

Shouted

The court heard West had previously:

● **THROWN** a dining table out of an upstairs window.

● **SHOUTED**, sworn and waved the wheel rims round in a public library, and

● **VANDALISED** a fish and chip shop when told there nothing on the menu for 10p.

West was jailed for 11 months by Judge Dermod O'Brien, QC, after being found guilty of indecent assault, and admitting deception, making off without payment and damaging a table.

VEGGIE *Malcolm Coates*

Hubby hops it to rabbit hutch in his salad daze

BURLY joiner Malcolm Coates got so fed up being fed salads by his missus, he built a giant rabbit hutch ... and MOVED IN!

He began his potty protest as a joke. But he loved his new life so much, he went BUNNY BARMY, worried friends revealed.

Meat-loving Malcolm has now gone veggie, takes his furry friends to work with him — and sups CARROT JUICE in his local boozer!

"I can't deny it," he said last night. "Those fluffy bobtails have made my life complete."

Feeding

Malcolm, 30, of Baddeley Green, Stoke-on-Trent, said: "I used to believe a man should eat meat when he wanted a REAL meal.

"But my wife Helen said I should lose a bit of weight for the summer and started feeding me salads day in, day out."

So he knocked up his huge hutch in the back garden and slept in it for a laugh with the family's pet rabbits.

But when he felt the cuddly bunnies snuggling up to him for warmth, his life was TRANSFORMED.

PUSSIES IN BOOT

POSH moggies in Paris have a purr-fect way of getting about ... their own dial-a-cab service launched by a taxi firm which also carries dogs.

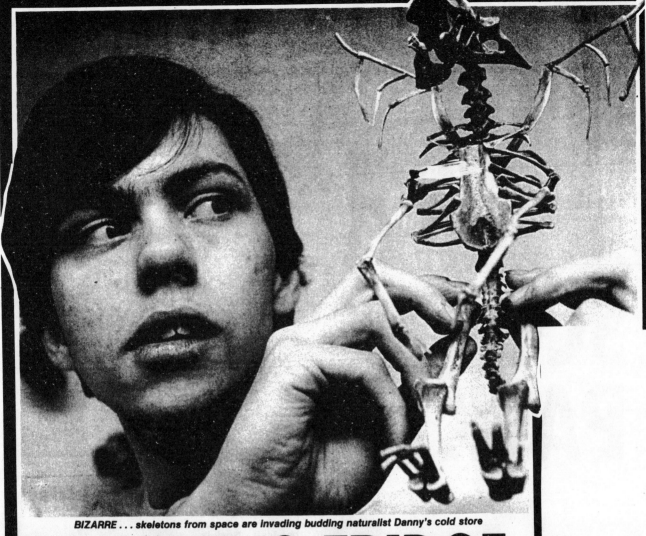

BIZARRE . . . skeletons from space are invading budding naturalist Danny's cold store

PRINTER'S FRIDGE TURNS INTO ALIEN GRAVEYARD

MILD-MANNERED Danny Grundy last night told how his fridge-freezer has been turned into an ALIENS' GRAVEYARD!

The 20-year-old printer keeps his amazing collection of ET SKELETONS — beamed down from biscuit tin-shaped spaceships — next to the yoghurt and cheese.

His cache of bones from beyond Earth is

MYSTIFIED . . . Grundy

By RAY LEVINE

growing by the month as more carcases mysteriously materialise in his cold store.

Holding a bizarre-shaped skeleton, Danny said: "This was the first specimen. I found it one morning next to the freezer compartment.

Boffins

"That was last year and I've had dozens since," he added.

Now boffins at the Natural History Museum are preparing to examine his ASTON-ISHING finds.

Skeletons of an EIGHT-inch wide "spider," a rat-sized "dino- saur" and a foot-long "flea," are sitting on the top shelf of Danny's fridge.

The budding naturalist, from Bolton, Lancs, says the mysterious beasts are sent by spacemen from a distant planet.

He claims it's their way of introducing humans to the odd animals which inhabit their world before they APPEAR on Earth!

"Judging by the skeletons, these animals would look very odd to us. So it follows the life forms sending them must look odd, too," he said.

Danny believes he was chosen to look after the skeletons after a close encounter with a spaceship.

The silent 60-foot craft hovered above his head and bathed him in a GREEN LIGHT before whizzing off.

"I can't think of any other reason why these bones started appearing in my fridge.

Weird

Sunday Sport boffins confirmed Danny's skeletons look like nothing on Earth.

The WEIRD alien artefacts will shortly be taken to the museum for closer analysis.

A museum spokesman said: "We cannot speculate on where these bones come from but it sounds an interesting case."

● THE world's only surviving ALIEN EGG on earth was rescued from the Russians last year and is currently being held in a secret underground bunker... where boffins reckon it will hatch SOON!!

● SUNDAY SPORT stunned the world last year when we exclusively revealed how a West Country man sensationally discovered an ALIEN FOSSIL — believed to be millions of years old — in his BACK GARDEN!!

HUNGRY SQUIRREL ATE MY SCOUT PACK

WILD LIFE SHOCK FOR TROOP

Bushy monster blows his nut on woggle boys

By BERTIE 'Dib Dib' OLLOCKS

STUNNED scoutmaster David Reid went NUTS last night, after hearing how his troop was savaged by a giant KILLER SQUIRREL!

The tufty terror SLASHED the screaming sprogs with razor-sharp claws, then tried to GNAW off their heads.

The blood-crazed bushy-tail launched its FRENZIED attack while the lads strolled on a carefree nature ramble in the leafy Norfolk woodland near Kelly Heath.

MARK...he saw rodent

The rampant rodent was finally beaten off with a walking stick.

Scout Mark Prentice, 15, said last night: "I was convinced it was going to KILL us.

"It happened as we were walking. There were five of us camping out as part of a Scout badge test."

Streaked

Mark, of Lowestoft, Suffolk, added: "We heard a rustling noise in a bush and went to investigate.

"Suddenly, this huge shape as big as a dog streaked out of the leaves and launched itself at us."

Mark, who belongs to the First Kessingland Scout troop, said the mutant monster launched several attacks and followed them when they tried to run away.

"It went completely mad," he said.

MOVE OVER, ROVER

HENPECKED hubby Harry Payne was forced to sleep in the DOG-HOUSE when his wife's pet Doberman dog moved into his bed in Toronto, Canada.

BAGPIPES TRIED TO BLOW ME AWAY

CRAZED KILLER BAG IN HORROR ATTACK ON MARK

By SIMON FINLAY

BURLY builder Mark Bilton will spend New Year's Eve plastered . . . after being attacked by KILLER BAGPIPES.

In an amazing pre - Hogmanay horror, muscleman Mark was hurled down a flight of stairs by the ferocious pipes—which came to LIFE and CHASED him round the house.

Last night, bruised Mark, a broken ankle in plaster, warned revellers all over Britain: "The crazed pipes are still on the LOOSE!"

He told how the manic music bag shrieked a SPINE-CHILLING version of Amazing Grace before springing to life and attacking him.

"It kept BASHING me over the head with its air-bag—it was terrify-

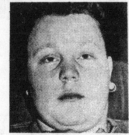

TERRIFIED . . . Mark

ing," claimed Mark—who borrowed the pipes for a New Year's Eve knees-up.

"I made a break for the door—but the pipes tripped me nd I tumbled down the stairs. That's how I bust my ankle."

"I'd borrowed the bagpipes to entertain some Scottish mates at New Year," said unemployed Mark—who faces eight weeks in plaster.

Ripped

"I came back from the pub and decided to have a quick practice on the pipes before turning in for the night.

"I went to sleep and the next thing I knew, the pipes were all over me. They had JUMPED onto the bed, RIPPED back the bedclothes and were BUTTING me with the airbag.

"It was sort of using its pipes as LEGS—it could really move!" added Mark.

"I know I'd had a few Christmas drinks down the pub — but I'm sure I wasn't seeing things.

PAGE 3 BEAUTY'S SECRET SIZE 18⅞ FEET

TOE-HOLD

Belinda loves to model . . . but always insisted her plates of meat stayed well out of camera range . . . until yer super Sunday Sport gave her the chance to reveal all.

REVEALED! Why top stunnas are NEVER shown below-the-belt

GREAT BRITISH EXCLUSIVE

BUSTY Belinda Trotter last night revealed the best kept secet of British models . . . their over-sized FEET.

As millions drool over Page Three stunners—but NEVER see their tootsies —Belinda unveiled her own and declared: "Bet you've never seen whoppas like these!"

Brighton beauty Belinda, 19, has kept her size 18⅞ plates of meat under wraps throughout her glamour career.

"People don't realise that we ALWAYS keep our feet off camera," confided Belinda.

"Lots of girls are embarrassed by their titanic tootsies . . . but I guess mine are just that bit extra-special."

Belinda added: "Now you can see why I'm called Bigfoot on the modelling circuit!"

FULL STORY PLUS AMAZING PHOTOS —CENTRE PAGES

Anglers fear for fingers as outbreak of killer fish hits rivers

By BERTIE OLLOCKS

PETRIFIED anglers across Britain are living in terror of a shoal of giant, mutant KILLER FISH.

The soggy horrors infest secluded, leafy riverbanks, waiting to feast on HUMAN FLESH.

For the piranha-like predators lurking in the backwaters have burst out of a trout farm where theyn were fed on a gut-wrenching diet of high-protein pellets.

Razor-toothed giants have wiped out river life on several waterways...now they are lying in wait for the fishermen themselves.

Keen angler Tony Longstaff, of Farnborough, Hants, was among the first victims.

Razors

He said last night: "I thought I had a real beauty on the line, but when I tried to land it, the monster took a chunk out of my finger.

I'd never seen anything that size before. It's teeth were like razors. The pain was agonising. People must be warned."

His friend Ronnie Murray, who witnessed the incident, said: "They are eating everything in their path. They are covering with festering sores because they are unused to river-borne bacteria.

"I would hate to see them end up on anyone's dinner plate."

Wizard way to aid world

WITCHES plan to cast an amazing spell — to save the earth's ozone layer!

It's part of a bizarre magic masterplan from the UK-based Covenant Of Earth Magic.

White magic bosses have urged disciples to link up on Hallow'ean — to protect the environment.

The occultists plan to flash psychic messages warning world leaders about the damage pollution is causing to the earth's atmosphere.

Bird ops on cheap

A BARMY bird boffin claims to have SUCK-SEEDED in perfecting an operation . . . for tubby BUDGIES.

The vet, from Oslo, Norway, is chirpin all the way to the bank by carrying out CHEAP fat-trimming ops on the bulky birds.

Flustered budgie lovers are flocking to his door — after their pets gobble down so much seed they can't fly.

The vet is now feathering his own nest, claim sceptics.

FASHION QUEEN'S HAIRY HELL

Cindy's torment uncovered at last . . .

BRISTLING beauty Cindy Bush last night got her astonishing secret agony off her chest . . . she's covered with HAIR.

Stunning Cindy, 21, turned her life into a series of close shaves to stop the modelling world finding out. But now the gorgeous French-woman—known as Sophie DuBois in glossy mag circles—has made a clean breast of her hell.

MORE AMAZING PICTURES: Centre Pages

OR BEAUTY *Cindy turns the fellas' heads after a face-saving close shave*

PRINCE CHARLES IN ALIEN KIDNAP SHOCK

PRINCE Charles has been insured for £5 million... against being KIDNAPPED by SPACE ALIENS.

And the insurers have promised to pay Princess Di DOUBLE if Charles is EATEN or given a dose of SPACE AIDS BY THE ETs.

The policy was hand-delivered to the wacky Royal at his office in St James Palace, London.

The bizarre contract promises to cover costs of psychiatric treatment, with a double indemnity clause "if the aliens refer to the abductee as a nutritional food source," or if the aliens "refuse to practise SAFE SEX".

Orders for the policies, provided by the UFO Abduction Insurance Company, have been flooding in.

Customers include oddball movie queen Shirley MacLaine, US chat show host Johnnie Carson and dozens of clients of top British underwriters Lloyds of London.

And the company has already agreed to PAY UP after one customer PROVED she was bundled aboard a space-ship by aliens.

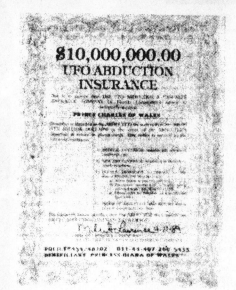

$10,000,000.00 UFO ABDUCTION INSURANCE

By JOHN GARVEY

Company boss Mike St Lawrence, 41, said last night: "We were very pleased to provide coverage for the future King of England."

Businessman Mike opened the company in 1987 after his brother Dennis, 37, was kidnapped by aliens and was beamed back down to find he had no insurance cover against the unlikely event.

PROOF... policy

Now the American firm, based in Florida, has a huge turnover and has sold thousands of five million dollar policies.

"And we stand by our word. One 86-year-old lady has already successfully claimed. We have promised to pay at the rate of one dollar per year for the next ten million years.

But Mike has become a victim of his own success. American Express have threatened to take out an injuction to prevent him using the slogan: "Don't leave Earth without It," which is similar to their own catchphrase.

■ TEENAGER Peter Crawley has been thrown in at the deep end after landing a job at Doncaster Museum – he has to weigh 60 pickled newts a day.

How he loved his pedigree chum

MAN EATS DOG — THAT'S A REAL TALE

TOUGH oil-man Jim "Tex" Ford couldn't bear to be without his dog Shanka when he died — so he made him into a stew and ATE him.

He told the tough roustabouts working on building North Sea oil rigs with him: "It's not sick or cruel . . . I'm doing it for love."

"My God, I loved that dog," bachelor Jim told me. "I ate him because that way he'll be a part of me forever."

Shanka, a black and white Border Terrier, met his end at the age of five in a fight with an Alsatian and died in Jim's arms in Peterhead, Aberdeenshire.

"I talked to him like a friend and we made a pact that whatever happened we would be buried together," said Jim 52.

"I cried like a baby, but I kept my promise. The only way I could make sure I was buried with my faithful friend was to take him with me . . . so I ate him, with lots of salt and pepper.

By Marion Scott

"I skinned him and I boiled him.

"When my mates found out they were horrified and called me names. But I don't think I did anything wrong."

Jim's now got a new pal, a whippet called prince.

"I wear Shanka's pelt as a belt round my trousers," he said. "He was more a friend than any human being. I know he'd approve."

With the decline in the oil industry, Jim has decided to try his luck as a roadbuilder. He hopes hard work will help him get over the loss of his pedigree chum.

Hot dog collared

BRUCE the Collie found himself in the hot seat after he was left alone in a car.

For the clever canine climbed into the driving seat — and started the engine.

Police in Littlehampton, Sussex, were called and Bruce was "collared".

His owner, Ian Gardener from Tilehurst, Berks, said: "Goodness knows how he started the engine but fortunately the police saw the funny side of it."

1 IN 7 PEOPLE IS A

WE'VE GOTTA HEAD 'EM OFF

ALIEN...not like this

THEY'RE HERE! *This amazing picture, taken at a London railway station this week, shows the eerie glow around the heads of commuters which scientists say is proof they are not human ... but aliens amongst us*

SPACE ALIEN

10 WAYS YOU CAN EXPOSE AN ALIEN

1 Never drinks anything in public.

2 Has pointy ears and GREEN blood.

3 ALWAYS wears space suit to fancy dress parties.

4 He glows in the dark.

5 He has a satellite dish but no TV.

6 Stargazes 'cos he's homesick.

7 Cuts himself shaving to reveal green scales.

8 Got a spaceship in his backyard.

9 Missus doesn't have any babies — she lays eggs.

10 Reads Sunday Sport to catch up on 'home affairs.'

THIS earth-shattering picture was hailed last night as positive PROOF that up to one in seven people are SPACE ALIENS!

It was taken with a radiation-sensitive camera at a London rail station last week.

And it shows an EERIE GLOW round the heads of commuters.

The classified snap — leaked to Sunday Sport — could prove ETs are LIVING AMONG US.

Out of the 84 people within thee terminal, 12 emitted the strange aura. Last night, leading

By BERTIE OLLOCKS
Our man who's spaced out

paranormal researcher Paul Eyles said: "This could confirm what many people have long supported — the ALIEN INVASION has already HAPPENED.

"Although they will NEVER admit it, the military have been working on this hypothesis for some time.

Secrecy

"If these beings can successfully MASQUERADE as humans, at home and at work, they are so advanced there seems little we can do but wait and see what their purpose is

— whether it is for GOOD or EVIL."

Scientists initially believed, however improbable, the GLOWING figures may have been exposed to RADIATION. They enlisted official help to trace them.

Intelligence experts worked overtime and found the "ordinary" people could largely be identified.

But they were STUNNED to discover that the HALOED figures were literally untraceable...

Swiss scientist Prof

Hugo Kornhelm, 68, who claimed his own government had sworn him to secrecy, broke ranks last night and told our investigators:

"It is the opinion of myself and colleagues that the people in your picture are NOT HUMAN."

A British colleague of Prof Kornhelm's who insisted his name was not disclosed, said: "I can CONFIRM what you have been told.

"It caused quite a scare. Intelligence bods at the Defence Ministry set about tracing them — but couldn't.

"The only conclusion to be drawn is: THEY'RE NOT HUMAN!"

HITLER'S BONES FOUND ON BRIT BEACH

HITLER'S remains—including his SKULL—have been washed up on Brighton beach, experts claim.

And, as our AMAZING snapshot shows, the evil monster was defiant to the end—one bone raised in a final Nazi SALUTE.

Amazed scientists now believe the gay psychopath may have SURVIVED the war—and ended his days in Britain.

Using revolutionary new technology, scientists reconstructed features belonging to the skull.

Their computer-generated image bears a CHILLING likeness to the most hated man in history.

A stunned Oxbridge boffin said last night: " If this find is genuine, we'll have to RE-WRITE the history books!"

The devilish discovery was made by holidaying Scottish student Michael Grant, 24.

He sent the remains along with this SENSATIONAL snapshot —to top forensic doctor Gillian Doran.

" I was shaken to the core when I discovered who it was. I don't think I'll ever get over it," said stunned Dr. Doran.

FULL INVESTIGATION CENTRE PAGES . . .

SIEG HEIL *Hitler's grisly remains give a last defiant salute on sunny Brighton beach*

MEATY STORIES ABOUT THE OLD SOUR KRAUT...

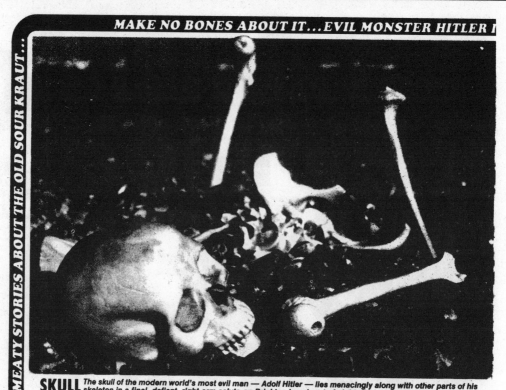

SKULL The skull of the modern world's most evil man — Adolf Hitler — lies menacingly along with other parts of his skeleton in a final, defiant, right arm salute on Brighton beach out of sight of pleasure seekers

BRIGHTON SHOCKER

WHAT MAKES AN IRON CROSS? BEING BENT AND GETTING TOO HOT, OF COURSE...

HITLER'S WASHED BRITISH

A SKULL washed up on Brighton beach has been reconstructed into the spitting image of Nazi butcher ADOLF HITLER . . . and top historians are doing their NUT about it.

The cranium and bones—discovered nestling in driftwood and pebbles yards from the resort's famous pier—were thought, at first, to be the remains of a MURDER victim.

But a dramatic rebuilding of the bones and flesh by forensic scientists has revealed the chilling features of this century's most

EVIL mass KILLER —who was last seen alive in 1945.

Now boffins are speculating over the circumstances of the crazed Kraut leader's death—and the historians may have to REWRITE history.

Respected

"I was STUNNED when I saw the results of the reconstruction. I could barely believe the likeness to Hitler," said leading independent forensic expert Dr. Gillian Doran, after FLESHING OUT the sea-worn skull.

"When I drew the artist's impression from the studies I'd made, I felt a SICKNESS in my gut," she added.

The skull was found by

By BILL PEARCE
Our man at the seaside

medical student Michael Grant, 24, while on holiday.

Respected Canadian scientist Dr. Doran—who has devoted her life to studying human remains —spent days checking her findings before coming to the awful truth.

"I'm convinced it's Hitler's skull. I spent lots of time poring over old pictures and newsreels to see if there was anything in Hitler's appearance which might sway me from my conclusion," she added.

"The skull fits Hitler's profile in every respect."

The amazing revelations come almost 45 years to the week since the MAD-DOG Fuhrer, then 56, disappeared into a German bunker when he knew the

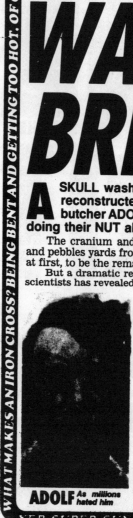

ADOLF As millions hated him

Love storey for Thomas

TOYBOY bridegroom Thomas Schwartz has shocked his relations by tying the knot with a 90-year-old HOUSE!

It was love at first sight when the besotted bachelor first saw the three-storey home he calls Victoria Hanover.

Thomas — a 33-year-old computer boffin — wed Victoria in a front-garden service attended by close friends under the watchful eyes of curious neighbours, in Des Moins, Iowa, USA.

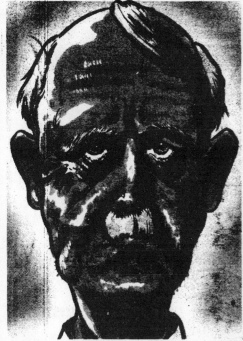

AND *This is how Hitler would have looked today, aged 101, after an artist used the skull to pick out his features*

SKULL UP ON BEACH!

CROSSBONES *This match of skull and Fuhrer proves the gay womaniser ended as just another pebble on the beach — stone dead*

Why he's by ...

■ THERE are four theories how Hitler's bones were washed up.

■ ONE: CLOSE aides may have DUMPED the body in the sea AFTER the Fuhrer killed himself.

■ TWO: SS guards concocted the "burning" of bodies outside the Berlin bunker but their getaway boat was gunned down and Hitler DROWNED.

Sieg Heil – side

■ THREE: The Nazi leader's body was DROPPED from a German plane off the French coast in a bid to escape Allied advances.

■ FOUR: Hitler's death was fabricated and he lived happily for many years among the gay community of Brighton, and dropped dead during a stroll on the beach and was washed out to sea.

bodies has NEVER been discovered. That they were disposed of in some way remains a POSSIBILITY.

Dr. Doran reckons the bones she has been studying are at least 40 years old. But she's not sure how long they have been in salt water.

"*The sea may have helped to keep the bones in some sort of preserved state, but they are likely to have been in there for a very long time.*"

Rumours

Shirer, in his famous record of the Nazi tyranny, admits: "The bones were never found and this gave rise to rumours after the war that Hitler had SURVIVED."

Dr. Doran's methods of building up a picture of a dead person is used widely in criminal forensic science ... and genetic scientists are stripping old bones for clues.

And Dr. Doran said: "The one good thing to come of all this is that we know Hitler is DEAD for SURE. Any rumours or speculation he may be still alive are now WORTHLESS.

"At least, that HORRENDOUS thought can be completely discounted if the rest of the world accepts my theory," she added.

second World War was lost.

He was never seen again —and historians believed rumours he'd blown out is BRAINS.

But, although jackbooted SS goons are said to have carried the Nazi leader's body—along with his wife Eva Braun's corpse—to a funeral pyre near the Berlin bunker, *no trace was ever found of the bones.*

No evidence he shot himself

The history books all quote identical "eyewitness" accounts of how the bodies were placed on the bonfire, doused with petrol and TORCHED.

But Dr. Doran reckons there WOULD have been remains of the bodies because the fire would not

have been hot enough to reduce the bodies to ashes.

Respected books like The Rise and Fall of the Third Reich by William Shirer and Hitler: A Study In Tyranny by Alan Bullock, both have no concrete explanation of what happened to the bones or the ashes.

"The simplest explanation is Hitler's body was never burned and perhaps he didn't even shoot himself. Eva Braun poisoned herself—so it's possible HE did TOO, said Dr. Doran.

"There is no evidence in the remains I have that he shot himself," she added.

Dr. Doran was sent the remains by visiting Scottish student Michael after he stumbled on the skeleton during a morning stroll.

Using a complicated and lengthy process of studying

relative skin depths and calculating the age of the bone tissue, Dr. Doran was able to pick out certain features.

"I was able to etch each detail as I went along. Michael told me he'd kept it for six months to use as a study aid and he seemed keen to know more about my findings," said Dr. Doran.

Sea may have preserved bones

She added: "One day, he phoned me—the day I was finally sure of the identity. When I told him, the line went DEAD.

Top historians agree the remains riddle is one of the unsolved parts of the story about Hitler's death.

In his 1952 book, Alan Bullock wrote: "What happened to the burned

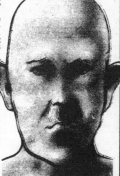

BUST *A plaster bust was made from the skull*

■ OUR second artist's impression is derived from the plaster bust made from the invaluable information collected by Dr Doran.

■ Her team of assistants used the Fuhrer's unique bone structure to show his crooked nose, high cranium and square chin.

Your pet may be psychic

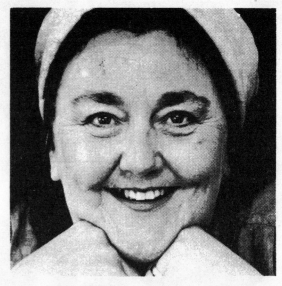

SENSATIONAL . . . Anne's pet powers

Says Britain's No 1 Psychic Anne Owen

TOP psychic Anne Owen today continues her sensational series on mind-power and asks: "Does your PET know what you're thinking?"

For, after an incredible investigation by the world's greatest medium, she has found that dogs, cats, mice, hamsters and even GOLDFISH have mind-bending psychic abilities.

And Anne exclusively reveals how to tell if your pet is telepathic and explains the ways you can CHAT to it by THOUGHT.

Clairvoyant Anne reckons 90 per cent of British people — around 50 million of us — have psychic powers without realising it.

But she claims our PETS have even greater uncanny powers of telepathy and fortune telling.

"One surefire way of finding out if YOUR pet is psychic is to take him on an expedition to an old house or some other spooky place that is supposed to be haunted," says the mystic mother-of-two.

"If he whines pathetically and refuses to go near, he is trying to tell you something. Reassure him and leave smartly, if he isn't already towing you away."

Anne insists psychic pet incidents are more common than many folk believe.

"There was the well-known case of a little boy who disappeared into a narrow cave in Majorca," she said.

"His pet Irish setter, called Harpo, was at home as the boy's family held a cliff-top picnic unaware he was helplessly trapped.

"Later, a frantic police search was called off after two days when all hope faded for the missing youngster.

"But when the boy's distraught parents arrived home the dog charged more than a mile back to the cliffs and whined outside the entrance to the tiny, concealed cave.

"Inside, the boy's father found his son — unconscious but still alive.

● If you have a psychic experience through Sunday Sport, tell Anne all about it by writing to her c/o Psychic Miracle, Sunday Sport, 3rd Floor, Marten House, 39-47 East Road, London N1 6AH.

If you can't wait, ring 01-608 0026 on Monday between 10am and 6pm.

Monster toads in Oz baby terror

BABIES are being mauled by a plague of giant killer cane TOADS.

Millions of the monsters are hopping across Australia EATING everything in sight.

BAT'S CLEVER!

DRACULA docs in Transylvania have discovered an anti-clotting chemical which could stop heart attacks . . . in vampire bats' saliva!

Stake-out for sicko attacker

A VAMPIRE mugger has bitten off fingers, ears and noses from victims in Homestead, Florida. "It's just not human," said a worried cop. "But at least we've got the teeth marks to go on."

Sock stinker

STUDENT Olivier Champion, whose SOCKS caught fire at Gatwick Airport because he packed them near lighter fuel and matches, was fined by Crawley magistrates yesterday for endangering passengers.

RUBBER PLANTS SPROUT CONDOMS

Steve's French letter tree leaves botany boffins baffled

GREEN-FINGERED Steve Bowditch was cock-a-hoop last night, after each of his rubber plants produced a luvverly bunch of CONDOMS!

Stunned Steve was watering the potty plants when he noticed they were covered in strange shoots.

And when he checked next morning, he found contraceptives growing from every leaf.

"I could hardly believe my eyes," said the 27-year-old miner.

"At first, I thought it was my mates playing a practical joke. But, after I'd taken a closer look, I realised the things were actually GROWING!"

Steve reckons there could be a massive demand for the fruity fruits.

"Someone will have to use them. This lot would take me well into the New Year," he admitted.

"But some of the blokes I hang around with would use them in a week."

He added: "As I've got the first species of its type, I reckon I should name it," he said proudly at his Stoke-on-Trent home.

"It will be known as

AMAZED . . . Steve and his plant

By JON OGDEN

Contraceptive Stoppus Kiddius.

"I could put some ink in the feed to make BLACK ones, or cross-breed one of the plants with a fir tree and get a real TICKLER," he said.

Stoke-on-Trent museum's Natural History curator was baffled by the natural wonder.

"Although I know these plants contain rubbery sap, to have one which sprouts condoms is stretching a point," said Geoff Halfpenny.

HUBBY KEEPS WIFE FROZEN IN HIS BATH

Wotta R.I.P. roarin' romance this is...

EXCLUSIVE

HEARTBROKEN British hubby Mitchell Dunham last night confessed the CHILLING secret in his bathroom—he keeps his dead wife in the TUB.

Mitchell couldn't bear to be parted from his childhood sweetheart Ann when she died. So he's preserved her corpse in a bath of ice.

● FULL STORY – 16/17

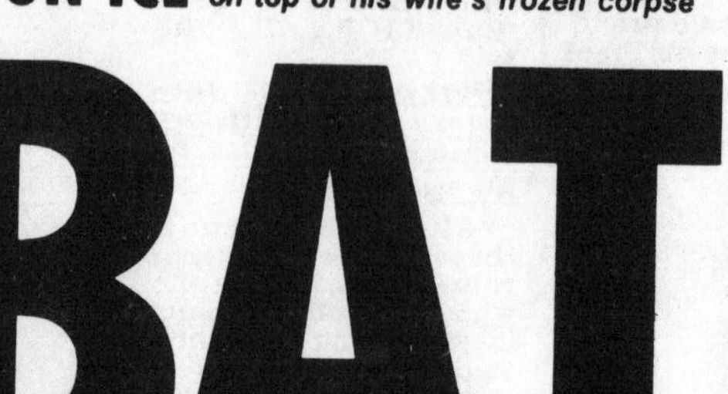

ON ICE Hearbroken Mitchell lays flowers on top of his wife's frozen corpse

CURRY BEEFS UP JOINER'S MANHOOD

...Fakir's curse led to monster

HOT *Warren's sprouting*

JUBILANT joiner Warren Prins claims he sprouted a MONSTER manhood ... by dipping his DONG in a CURRY!

Lucky Warren reckons his todger grew an extra TWO INCHES after he tipped the spicy slop into his underpants and went to sleep.

In a message that will give hope to millions he said last night: *"It really WORKS."*

"I marinated my manhood in a Madras — but any curry will do. The secret is in the SPICES."

Warren, 29, said his life was changed during a dream holiday to India, when a fakir took exception to him and CURSED him in a restaurant.

"The staff said my tool was going to DROP OFF within a week and roared with laughter."

Madras

"I got a bit worried and asked if there was anything I could do to prevent it."

They told him ...

"That night I closed the curtains and poured the whole Madras into my Y-fronts," said Warren, of Aldershot, Hants.

The next morning, he checked to see if his willie was intact — and was astonished to see a MONSTER beneath the sheets.

He said: "It was HUGE. I had to throw away my Y-fronts. But it's a small price to pay. I can't wait to get laid and try out my new weapon," he said.

MENU
Madras Curry

1. Fry a large onion;
2. Sizzle some mutton;
3. Add a spot of coriander, cumin, turmeric, chilli, ginger and garlic . . .
4. . . . half a pint of water, tomato puree, coconut and lemon juice;
5. Simmer for an hour.
6. Allow to cool, then tip into Y-fronts and leave to marinate for at least eight hours.

Sea find's amoozing!

SHOCKED scientists were scratching their heads last night...after finding a COW at the bottom of the OCEAN.

The boffins made the A-MOO-ZING find during routine research in a remote area off the Alaskan coast.

One expert said: "It may have fallen off a boat – it has not been there long judging by its condition."

HOOT

I CAN'T understand why everyone's fussing about Prince Charles just because he stuffs TOOTHPASTE up his hooter!

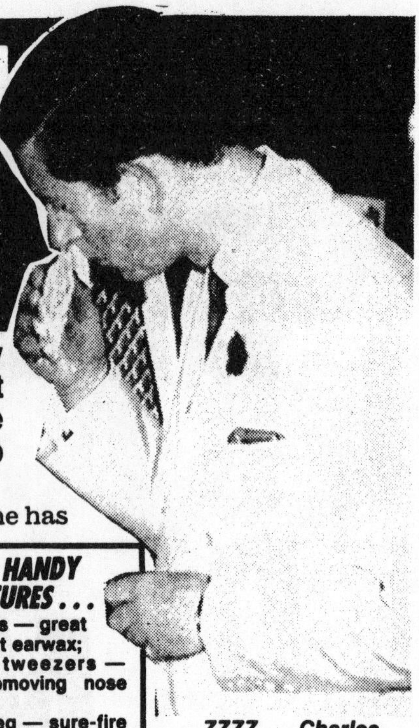

His admission this week that he has a ring of confidence where most people ram a hanky is actually another indication that our future King is . . . NORMAL.

Sure he's educated. Sure he's got more cash than a poll tax collector . . . but he's human too!

Exploit

That's why he was prepared to go to these bizarre lengths to stop himself snoring — and give Di a good night's sleep.

It's also reassuring to know that the man who's eventually going to govern the British people suffers a condition common to many . . . snoring.

Some unscrupulous observers will obviously try to exploit this human frailty . . . one newspaper even called him POTTY.

Well, I disagree. He's fit to rule because he's one of us . . . I just hope I never have to borrow his toothbrush.

10 HANDY CURES . . .

- Matchsticks — great for poking out earwax;
- Eyebrow tweezers — ideal for removing nose hairs;
- Clothes peg — sure-fire cure for snoring;
- Broom handle — strap to back and correct posture;
- Rubber gloves — stop anyone biting their nails;
- Chicken droppings — to stop you licking chapped lips;
- Milk bottles — they can draw out blackheads;
- Ice cubes — shove down the back to cure hiccups;
- Padded bra — effective earmuffs;
- The Sunday Sport — a cure for all ills!

ZZZZ . . . Charles

Mike munches pasta faster!

MIGHTY mouth Mike Harvey has chomped his way into the record books by eating 20 pounds of SPAGHETTI in just 15 minutes! Between contests Mike scoffs five chickens a day.

DOTTY SURF-IVER!

SHIPWRECKED fisherman Lotty Stevens, 18, hitched an incredible SIXTEEN day life-saving Pacific ride on a deadly STINGRAY!

SHELL SHOCKER

ANIMAL lovers in Charmouth, Dorset, have launched a campaign to protect part of the coastline—so SNAILS can BONK in peace.

NOT THRILLED

WACKY professor Lauren Harris is as sick as a parrot, having spent three years and £100,000 trying to discover why the birds eat LEFT-HANDED — and failed!

KILLER JOBBIE TURD ME INTO A ZOMBIE

EXCLUSIVE

By BERTIE OLLOCKS our Green correspondent

HORRIFIED swimmer Martin Bartlett sent shockwaves through the medical world last night with the amazing claim: "SMELLY SEWAGE turned me into a ZOMBIE!"

A dip in the briney changed to terror when he realised he was wading through a sea of BOBBING JOBBIES.

Next morning, his energy had gone, his head and throat ached and his eyes had puffed up into bags of PUSS!

Now Martin has claimed pollution is to blame for his bizarre condition.

Martin, 19, said: "I feel like a zombie. At first, I thought I was BLIND. My eyes were stuck with a mucous substance.

"When I tried pulling them open, it was like glue was sticking them together.

"The filth in the water had got in them. All this hot weather is a breeding ground for INFECTION in the water.

"My eyes were white with SCUM and there were pools of mucous beneath the lids."

Martin, of Bridport, Dorset, was swimming at nearby West Bay.

Wessex Water's West Bay sewage manager Martin Jones said: "There is a mile-long sea outfall pipe at West Bay which pumps out domestic waste from 30,000 homes."

Martin was prescribed medication to clear up his eye infection, but claimed a SECOND swimmer had suffered similar symptoms.

SEEING BLUE . . . Martin

BIG IDEAS . . .

SCIENTISTS claim the earth was once inhabited by GIANTS, after discovering 9ft high human skeletons in Mexico's Sierra Madre Mountains.

SOCCER YOB CRUSHED IN FLAB QUEENS' SEX DEN

Cabbie's trapped by 128st fat bags

DAZED yob Steve Harris told last night how he ended up black and blue after a bizarre three-in-a-bed romp at a World Cup sex den.

Cabbie Steve landed in hospital after bonking 128-stone

By GAZZA THOMPSON

hippo sisters Nina and Gina Grotti!

Astonished Steve, one of thousands of England fans in Cagliari, was CRUSHED by his fatso Italian lovers.

Full story–Pages 16/17

BUILDER GIVES BIRTH TO NINJA TURTLE

SHELL SHOCKER FOR DUMPER...

Animal boffins baffled

SHELL *The turtle dropped by Steve peeps over the loo*

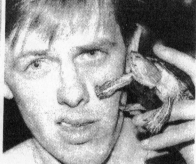

SHOCK *Steve looks at the creature he gave birth to*

By GAZZA THOMPSON

ZAPPED zoologists were SHELL-SHOCKED last night over builder Steve Thompson's amazing claim that he's given BIRTH...to a NINJA TURTLE!

The 22-year-old partition erector, from Essex, says the SLIMY REPTILE popped it's head out of his BACKSIDE when he went for a dump at his building site.

And he believes the heatwave could be responsible for an outbreak of THOUSANDS of bum-biting turtles across Britain.

"I went to lay a log in the bog and noticed the turtle swimming about in the pan," said Steve.

"I thought I must have eaten a dodgy curry or something because it was so painful. Then there was a loud RASPING sound and I saw the little creature.

"Me and some of the lads fished it out and stuck it in a box.

"The blokes on the site have called it Ninja because it keeps trying to BITE everyone."

MATE *Dave saw it after the birth*

Reptile

Steve's pal Dave Barnes, vouched for the batty birth. "I've seen it — it's a turtle," he said.

Stunned Steve — dubbed Reptile Pants by pals — says he had no idea he was carrying the crusty creature.

He claims he suffered severe CONSTIPATION for three days before being hit by an appalling attack of FLATULENCE!

"It felt like my bum was EXPLODING with enough force to pebble-dash a row of prefabs," said Steve, from Harlow.

His amazing revelations come in the week Britain has been hit by Turtlemania as the summer release of hit movie Teenage Mutant Ninja Turtles approaches.

Big crunch on the way

IT'S GONNA P**S DOWN CORNFLAKES

By BILL CORKE

FEARS mounted last night that a swirling CORNFLAKE TORNADO is heading for Britain!

Towns throughout America have already been blanketed in a crunchy carpet of flakes in a bizarre breakfast cereal fall-out.

Now weatherman predict the WACKY WHIRLWIND is whipping its way towards our shores.

"Strong westerly winds often carry lots of debris to Britain, after being sucked up on air currents," said a Met Office spokesman.

● **SNAP...** The first sighting of cornflakes falling from the sky was reported nearly a fortnight ago over Oklahoma.

● **CRACKLE...** Days later, a twister nicknamed Hurricane Munchy dropped thousands of bowlfuls of the flakes over a two-mile area New Mexico.

● **POP...** Only last week townsfolk in Nelson, Colorado, ran for cover as a cornflake blizzard brought traffic to a halt.

A spokeswoman for the makers of Kellogg's Cornflakes was STUNNED.

Studying

"I can't imagine where they're coming from, but I don't think they're ours," said Irene Jacques, at the company's Manchester headquarters.

● **HAS** anything strange ever rained down where YOU live? Write to "Pie-in-the-Sky," Sport Newspapers, Marten House, 39-47 East Road, London N1 6AH.

ALIEN KIDNAP

MORE than 5,000 Americans have taken out policies with the UFO abduction insurance company, based in Florida. They collect after being kidnapped by aliens.

THE BEST OF

SUNDAY SPORT

BUS FOUND

BURIED AT SOUTH POLE

NAUGHTY CARTOONS

"THE DIRTY OLD BUGGER'S ALWAYS SNEAKING LOOKS AT GIRLS PASSING BY IN THE STREET."

SPHERE